AMERICAN LABOR

FROM CONSPIRACY
TO
COLLECTIVE BARGAINING

INDUSTRIAL GOODWILL

John R. Commons

ARNO & THE NEW YORK TIMES
NEW YORK   1969

Reprint edition 1969 by Arno Press, Inc.

Library of Congress Catalog Card No. 75–89726

Manufactured in the United States of America

INDUSTRIAL GOODWILL

INDUSTRIAL GOODWILL

JOHN R. COMMONS
UNIVERSITY OF WISCONSIN

FIRST EDITION

SECOND IMPRESSION

McGRAW-HILL BOOK COMPANY, Inc.
239 WEST 39TH STREET. NEW YORK

LONDON: HILL PUBLISHING CO., Ltd.
6 & 8 BOUVERIE ST., E. C.
1919

THE MAPLE PRESS YORK PA

CONTENTS

INDUSTRIAL GOODWILL

I

COMMODITY

A few years ago I visited the employment office in a factory of several thousand workers. Scattered about were a number of sturdy immigrants fresh from the old country. On that day the manager was hiring Swedes. He said that the week before he had been hiring Poles, and before that he had taken on Italians. It was a good idea, he said, to get them mixed up. He told me of other large firms in that city with similar employment managers and a similar policy. They had an informal club that met usually once a week.

One of the things of which they were proud was their plan of forecasting the labor market. If labor was getting restless they could anticipate it by a concerted raising of wages 10 per cent until the storm blew over, and then reduce the wages back again, thus counteracting the work of agitators.

In order that they might be more accurately informed of the prospects of the labor market they had confidential arrangements with certain leaders of trade unions in the town, so that, if the unions were bringing organizers into the factories to stir

1

up unrest, the leaders would let them know in advance and would tell which establishments would be organized.

I visited one of the sidewalk offices of one of these establishments. A hundred men or so were assembled at the gate. The foremen were sending down their requisitions. The employment officer went along the line of the unemployed, looked at their feet, sized up their nationality and fitness, picked out ten or fifteen and sent them in. The others stood around with serious faces and then drifted away.

I went inside the factory. The raw material or semi-finished product was coming along on trolleys. One man performed one operation, another man another. Some highly skilled men in the gang were paid 50 cents an hour. Some of them seemed to be scarcely exerting themselves at all; others less adept were sweating. If any man did not do his part, the work piled up and he blocked the gang. The business of the foreman was, in part, to piece out the spots where men were not keeping up, or else fire the man and put in someone who could do it faster. Common laborers were on the jump, bringing in carts, carrying away the finished product.

Later I attended a meeting of strikers from that establishment. A Bohemian stood up and made a speech. By his side stood a Russian Jew who translated the speech into English. He pledged himself never to go back to work until their grievances were settled. He claimed that they could not make wages, that they had to work too hard, that they had to pay a bonus or make a present to the straw boss in order to keep the job. It seems that this strike started with a secret union of skilled men, and five thousand unskilled followed them out without an organization. It was a spontaneous strike without preliminary discussion in public. When they came together afterward for a joint meeting, it was necessary to have an interpreter whom they could trust. That man was the Russian Jew.

I went through the establishment and came across the strike-breakers. At noon time I found a group of Macedonians having a good time dancing and playing on a bag-pipe made of goat's skin brought from the Balkan Mountains. The padrone, who was in charge, could speak English, and told me of other towns where they had been used as strike-breakers. Negroes also were brought in, from the South. The strike was won, but immediately a second strike was called on account of alleged discrimination against the leaders. Naturally the company decided not to yield again. The men went back and their union went to pieces.

I visited some of these people at their homes and boarding houses. They were all eager to save money. That was their main ambition. At one boarding house was a big board table without any table cloth. In the middle of the table was a huge bowl. In that bowl were pork, cabbage, carrots, turnips, onions, a juicy steaming porridge. Each man at the table had his own smaller bowl. In the large bowl was a great ladle. A man reached over, filled his bowl and with his implements went to work. Beside this great bowl were huge loaves of bread. Each man would go after a loaf of bread, cut off what was about right and break it into his bowl. They were sturdy, vigorous peasants from the hill country of Europe.

Then I went into their sleeping rooms. One room was big enough to hold three double beds crowded together. In that room six men slept, and they crawled over one bed to get into the next one. They were saving money to send for their families or to go back and live.

When the family was here the mother was taking in boarders. We could now begin to talk to them without an interpreter. They would tell of their native country, its beauties, and tell something of the conditions, comparing their country with this. Usually the men seemed to earn about five times as much wages as they could earn in their home country, 20 cents a day there, $1.00 a day here. It would cost them about two or three times as much to live here as there, and they could save one-third to one-half of their wages.

It was their ambition to buy a home or get a farm. Recently I talked with the immigration agent of the state of Wisconsin. His business is to go to great manufacturing centers and find the type of man who has saved up enough money to buy a farm. For eight or ten years he has frequently seen something like the following. These people have worked for a number of years saving up money. The boy has gone to work, brought home money, which they have put in the bank. The girl is working in a factory or store. She has turned in her savings, and they have accumulated quite a sum of money. They see an advertisement in one of the foreign language papers. They learn of glowing possibilities at some place in

Wisconsin or other state. They connect up with that place and its land agent. They buy the farm. They place a mortgage on it or sign a land contract. They go on the farm, find a sandy soil, with much clearing to be done. They work it a year or so and use up their money. The mortgage is foreclosed and they scatter back to the city. It is the business of this immigration agent of the state of Wisconsin to protect these people from being defrauded when they buy and settle, and this he is doing in many cases, but in others he is thwarted by the old style of land agent.

When these settlers go back to the city, they must have work. They go to a private employment office. The employment man describes in attractive terms a job where they will find work. They pay a fee and pay for transportation. Recently, at one town in Wisconsin, thirteen of these people were landed, sent there for fake jobs. The town authorities had to send them back to the city. Finally, these people become migratory workers. It is estimated that of the migratory workers in this country 50 per cent are foreign born.

This is the workings of what I call the commodity theory of labor. Demand and supply determine wages. You cannot overcome the law of demand and supply. If labor is scarce, wages will go up. If labor is abundant, wages will go down. The ebb and flow of the labor market is like the ebb and flow of the commodity market.

I suppose it is true that you cannot overcome the law of supply and demand. But you can see how it works. The commodity theory of labor is perhaps the natural way for the merchant to look at it. He sits in his office, sends out his orders, buys finished commodities, buys in the cheapest market, sells in the dearest. He does not necessarily see his commodities. He can usually buy and sell by samples. Other people might look at it differently. A member of the engineering profession, for example, might naturally look on labor, not as a commodity, but as a machine.

II

MACHINERY

That which is bought and sold is not labor but the product of labor. If the worker is paid by the day or week it is usually because his product cannot be accurately measured. If he is paid by the piece the employer knows exactly what he is buying and how much he is paying for it. Piece-work furnishes accurate knowledge of labor costs and estimates of future costs.

Furthermore, piece-work stimulates the worker to greater exertion and attention. The rough, traditional estimate is 25 per cent greater output when paid by the piece than when paid by the day.

But this greater output has many individual differences. One man earns more than another at the same piece-rate. The foreman's business is to increase output and keep down costs. I knew a large factory of non-union laborers where every new man who came in was warned by the others not to earn more than a certain amount of money.

I knew another where two or three ambitious workers refused to limit their output on this mere warning from the others, and then the others organized a union, demanded the closed shop, won their demand, then reduced the output of every member so that no one would earn more than the amount of wages

7

that they thought the superintendent had in mind when he cut the piece-rates.

I knew still another where the president of the corporation vigorously denied in public that piece-rates were ever cut in his plant, and yet the foremen were cutting them right along.

These cases are not exceptional; they are only illustrations of what is universal. Indeed, piece-rates *must be cut*, sooner or later, or else either industry will stagnate, or wage-earners will get all of the gain from improvements and none will go to the consumer and the employer, or else the employer will be driven out of business by competition.

Piece-rate cutting is universal. What is meant when it is denied is perhaps that the cutting is not done *arbitrarily*. This is a question of fact, of definition, of opinion. The cutting must be done—the question is how and how often.

Twenty years ago many varieties of premium or bonus systems of paying wages began to be invented by engineers in order to abolish automatically the arbitrary cutting of piece-rates. Mr. F. S. Halsey, in 1902, stated the situation.[1] "From the nature of the day's-work plan the workman has no direct share in any increased production which he may bring about by more intelligent or increased exertion, the benefits of such increase going wholly to the employer. . . . From the nature of the piece-work plan, on the contrary, the employer has no direct share in any increased production which the workman may bring about by more intelligent or increased exertion. . . .

[1] *Sibley Journal of Mechanical Engineering*, Vol. XVI, March, 1902. Reprinted in Commons, *Trade Unionism and Labor Problems*, p. 274.

In consequence, community of interest between employer and employee in the reduction of costs is impossible. . . . It is this which it is the prime object of the premium plan to supply."

Mr. Halsey called the piece-work system a "system of punishment for doing well." The workman looks upon these cuts in piece-rates as "an exhibition of pure hoggishness on the part of the employer," but they are, he says, "an integral part of the piece-work plan, which can no more be operated without them than a windmill can be operated without wind, for the reason that as the years go by the whole tendency of prices is downward."

The premium plan, with its various modifications under the name of "bonus," "differential piece-rates" and so on, have this feature in common, that they are designed automatically to split the difference between the workman's desire for a minimum wage and the employer's desire for a maximum output.

The workman has certain minimum costs of living determined by his standard of living and the customs of the class with which he associates. Like the coal and oil and wear and tear of a machine, these must be met, no matter how inefficient he may be. So, the minimum wage per day is guaranteed, even though the product at the piece-rate would yield less than that minimum.

On the other hand, if every one is paid this minimum, there is no direct inducement for a man of ability and ambition to exceed it. Yet the ambitious man does not need as high a rate as the uniform piece-rate in order to induce him to exceed it. Furthermore, the employer also needs inducement to lead him to fix up his machinery and organization so that the workman will exceed the minimum. Hence the differential piece-rate, the bonus, or the premium on increased output, so that the worker and the employer may share between them the gain from increased efficiency. The worker gets his minimum wage and a bonus for extra output. The employer gets a lower average cost in wages the larger the bonus or premium earned by the worker.[1] Community of interest is automatically established. The foreman's inducement to cut the piece-rate has been eliminated, because the rate has already been cut by agreement in advance. The workman's inducement to increase his output is assured, for, by accepting something less than the old piece-rate, he does not expect to be punished for earning it.

[1] Mr. Halsey gives the following illustration of the workings of the premium plan where the workman is paid a minimum of $3.00 a day of ten hours, during which he produces 1 piece, and is paid a premium of 10 cents for each hour saved. Of course, the "premium" on *hours saved for a given product* works out the same as a "bonus" on amount of *product increased for a given number of hours.*

THE WORKINGS OF THE PREMIUM PLAN

1	2	3	4	5
Time consumed, hours	Wages per piece	Premium	Total cost of work = Column 2 + Column 3	Workman's earnings per hour = Column 4 ÷ Column 1
10	$3.00	$0.00	$3.00	$0.30
9	2.70	0.10	2.80	0.311
8	2.40	0.20	2.60	0.325
7	2.10	0.30	2.40	0.343
6	1.80	0.40	2.20	0.366
5	1.50	0.50	2.00	0.40

Commons, *Trade Unionism and Labor Problems*, p. 279.

There are two variables in this ingenious industrial psychology. First is the base rate, which we call the task; second is the bonus or premium rate for exceeding the task.

The early industrial psychologists, like Mr. Halsey, directed attention to the bonus rate. They were endeavoring to find a plan by which to lessen the temptation of the employer to cut the piece-rate. So they cut it in advance by making the premium rate say, 50 per cent or 30 per cent of the basic piece-rate. The straight piece-rate would be a bonus rate of 100 per cent on the base rate. But if the bonus rate is 50 per cent of the base rate, then the temptation to cut it is reduced 50 per cent. If the bonus rate is 30 per cent of the straight piece-rate, then the temptation to cut it is reduced 70 per cent, and so on.

This psychology turned out to be misdirected, and the premium system as thus portrayed broke down. The temptation to cut the rate did *not* reside in the *bonus* but in the *task*. I knew an establishment which introduced this premium system on an extensive scale. A man was given a job of say, 100 pieces at $3.00, and a bonus of 33⅓ per cent. If he doubled his output he would earn $4.00 a day and the labor cost to the employer would come down from 3 cents apiece to 2 cents apiece. But he went to work with ambition and ingenuity. He fixed up his machine and laid out his work. Eventually he was making some $7.00 a day. To do this he had increased his output, not two-fold, but five-fold. Then came the cut, *not* in the *bonus* rate but in the *task rate*. He received a surprise in the shape of a change in the job order. Instead of 100 pieces at $3.00 it became

200 pieces at $3.00, and the same bonus rate of 33⅓ per cent. He had to turn out twice as much product before he could begin to earn the bonus on extra product.

So the bonus rate is immaterial. The fear that the employer would cut the bonus rate was misplaced. The bonus rate is merely an inducement to exceed the task, and it makes but little difference whether it is 30 per cent or 50 per cent or even 100 or 150 per cent. The essential thing is the *base rate* which determines the task. This is just as essential in straight piece-work as it is in the premium or bonus system.

Here is where scientific management came in. Mr. Frederick Taylor made the next great step in advance. He directed his investigations, not to the bonus rate or premium rate, but to the task or base rate which should be required before the premium or bonus could begin. With the task correctly ascertained he even advocated a differential piece-rate as high as 150 per cent of the task rate as an inducement to exceed the output ascertained for the task, and a different rate, lower than the task rate, as an additional penalty for not coming up to the task.

With this new view of the matter we get back to the true nature of piece-work described by Mr. Taylor as a task-and-bonus system. Under the premium or bonus system the employer will not for long keep a workman who does not earn the minimum wage. The minimum wage becomes the task. The profitable employees are those who earn more than the minimum. The same is true on straight piece-work. Piece-work is also a task-and-bonus system, but with the bonus fixed at 100 per cent of the piece-rate.

But the task is uncertain. Mr. Taylor's great contribution to the subject was that of accurately *measuring* the *task* in advance, instead of leaving it to the hit-or-miss, cut-and-try, methods of the old style piece-work practice. Scientific management, applied to labor, is scientific measurement of the laborer's task required to hold the job.

With this new idea there is no difference between piece-work and the premium and bonus systems except in the very minor difference of the rate of premium. Whether it be Mr. Halsey's 33⅓ per cent or Mr. Taylor's 150 per cent, or even straight piece-work which is 100 per cent of the base rate, is a small matter. They are just different rates of premium or bonus on the amount of work a man does over the task. The task is the real thing and the only thing that needs scientific investigation.

The first practical application of this important distinction between the task and the bonus or premium was that of taking the authority to make piece-rates away from the foremen and placing it in the hands of investigators.

The foreman is not an inventor or investigator. He has come up from the ranks. He operates according to habit and tradition. He does not know much about the possibilities of improved processes and short cuts. More than that, he is busy in getting out product. He must get men to work and he must keep down costs. If he makes a mistake in setting the piece-rate too low he cannot get the workmen; if he sets it too high they will earn too much. It was these miscalculations that broke down the premium system as first applied, just as they had broken down the piece-work system which it was hoped the premium system would correct.

If the rate-fixing is taken away from foremen it can be placed in the hands of experts, inventors, investigators. They can study the possibilities of each job. They can study waste motions and short cuts. They can standardize the job according to the easiest and quickest method of doing the work. They can employ the accurate methods of measurement which distinguish science and engineering from rule-of-thumb. They can make time-and-motion studies, and set up specifications for the foreman and workman to follow. They can study each workman and select those who are fitted to each job.

This I call the machinery theory of labor. Labor is not a commodity—its value determined by demand and supply—but each laborer is a machine—its value determined by the quantity of its product. The theory is not new. Its application is a new discovery in science and engineering. The commodity theory is the merchant's theory of buying and selling. The machinery theory is the engineer's theory of economy and output. Man is, after all, the most marvelous and productive of all the forces of nature. He is a mechanism of unknown possibilities. Treated as a commodity, he is finished and ready for sale. Treated as a machine, he is an operating organism to be economized.

The application of this theory by the engineer is perhaps the most productive invention in the history of modern industry. The steam engine, electricity, chemistry, scientific agriculture, have done much to increase man's power over nature. But machinery and factory organization are continually approaching a limit of diminishing returns. This limit turns attention to the human factor, and it needs only a candid attention to the experiments of scientific management to become convinced of the large resources and unused possibilities within the human animal which can be developed when once his motions and energies are studied and measured as the engineer studies and measures the other forces and materials used in production.[1] It differs from the others in that the science of industrial psychology is added to the mechanical and biological sciences, and inducement is nicely adjusted to output through ingenious measurements of compensation.

Other inventions and improved processes have been opposed and resisted in the past by workingmen, just as this is more or less resisted. But if we may judge by what has happened in the past, the cheaper and more productive processes will win out by the mere force of competition. The workingmen who resist successfully gain an empty victory, for their employers cannot compete with the others, and while they gain their point for a time, they lose their jobs eventually.

Their resistance is logical, for scientific management carries to the final limit that disintegration of the workman's skill and its transfer to the employer, which began a hundred and fifty years ago with the inventions of power machinery, the steam engine, and division of labor. The ancient craft gilds were rightly known as "mysteries." The member of the

[1] Especially the writings of Taylor, Gilbreth, Gantt, Emerson, Thompson.

gild learned through his apprenticeship a skill in manufacture unknown and unpractised by outsiders. This mystery was his vested right—his property against all the world. But when machinery or division of labor took the place of his skill, his property-right went with it to his employer who owned the machine.

Scientific management carries the process a step further. The time-and-motion studies, the blue prints and specifications, the detailed instructions how to do the work, become the property of the employer, and the mechanic no longer hands down by word of mouth and by example the mystery of his skill. Where mechanical inventions transferred ownership of skill to the employer through ownership of the machine, scientific management transfers it through blue prints and job studies made by a staff of engineers and specialists on the staff of the employer.

Naturally, as before, the mechanic resists, but insofar as scientific management materially reduces costs by increasing output this resistance will be gradually undermined and the mechanic will learn, as he has to some extent in the case of machinery, to recoup in other directions.

III

GOODWILL

The machinery theory, like the commodity theory of labor, is not false, it is incomplete. You cannot, it is true, overcome the law of supply and demand. But you can modify it, if you know how, within limits. You cannot permanently withstand those improvements which, by enlarging output, reduce costs, but you can limit the improvement itself at the point beyond which, if carried too far, it increases costs elsewhere more than it continues to reduce them. Successful business is always a scheme of finding that correct proportion of different factors which brings the largest net income from all of them together.

At the moment when scientific management was achieving an evident success, another source of cost, less tangible but equally important, began to receive scientific investigation. This attention came first, not from industry or engineers, but from the field of vocational education. The Vocation Bureau of Boston, unable to place its boys in permanent jobs where their training could be continued after leaving school, brought the matter before the employment agents of several corporations. Out of these conferences developed the Employment Managers' Association of Boston, with its scientific study of labor turnover.[1]

[1] *Bulletin of the United States Bureau of Labor Statistics*, Number 196, p. 42.

Spontaneously, elsewhere, this hitherto unmeasured cost of labor received attention, and when, by a bold stroke of genius rather than science, the Ford Motor Company doubled its wages, but nevertheless increased its profits by the mere reduction in cost of labor turn-over, it became evident to all that the intangible good-will of labor may be as profitable as the scientific management of labor.

The laborer is not only a productive machine, he is a customer. The employer is not only buying his time or his product, but is also selling to him a job where he can earn a living. The employer makes a certain investment on behalf of every customer and every employee. He furnishes something in exchange, and he not only wants that customer or worker to return, satisfied with his treatment, but also to spread the word and bring others. Goodwill is good reputation, and reputation is the collective opinion of those whose patronage is desired.

The engineer treats each laborer as a separate individual. This is indeed necessary and right, for he is such. One machine is not as good as another. One is fitted for one kind of work, another for another kind. Selection of individuals is the first step in scientific management. So it is in scientific goodwill. But it is more.

Scientific management picks out the individual and offers him the inducement of making more money. It separates him out from the group with which he has consciously or unconsciously, perhaps, identified himself. It cuts across the solidarity of labor as a class, unmindful that the laborers are competitors with each other, that they are buying jobs which they feel are limited in supply, and that their feeling of solidarity on this account reprehends the one who injures his fellows by lessening their chances for jobs, or who reduces the level of compensation for all by his self-seeking competition.

But the goodwill of labor is a collective goodwill that does not play one laborer against another, or the unemployed against the employed, or take advantage of the needs of a class, but acknowledges labor's solidarity of interest as well as the individual laborer's self-interest.

Scientific management, since it begins and ends with individuals separated from their fellows, has the defects of autocracy. It means government by experts. An expert comes into the factory and makes a study of the operations of the selected individual. That individual and his fellow-workers are much concerned about his time studies, his stop-watch, his cold calculations, which decide for them the amount of work that shall be portioned out for the task. But they cannot be consulted. They are objects to be investigated, not investigators.

But goodwill is reciprocity. It is not government at all, but mutual concession. It yields as much to the prejudices and passions, to the conservatism and even suspicions of patrons as it does to scientific knowledge of what is good for them. Goodwill is not necessarily a virtuous will, or a loving will, it is a beneficial reciprocity of wills, and whether there is really a benefit or really a reciprocity, is a matter of opinion and mutual good feeling as much as a matter of science.

Goodwill is productive, not in the sense that it is

the scientific economizing of the individual's capacities, but because it enlists his whole soul and all his energies in the thing he is doing. It is that unknown factor pervading the business as a whole, which cannot be broken up and measured off in motions and parts of motions, for it is not science but personality. It is the unity of a living being which dies when dissected. And it is not even the personality of a single individual, it is that still more evasive personality to which the responsive French give the name, *l'esprit de corps*, the spirit of brotherhood, the solidarity of free personalities.

It is this corporate character of goodwill that makes its value uncertain and problematical. A corporation is said to have no soul. But goodwill is its soul. A corporation owns its goodwill, and the value of goodwill is reflected in its stocks and bonds. It is the soul of a going concern, the value of the unity and collective personality that binds together all its parts in a living organism.

The engineer or employer can tell exactly what is the labor-cost of a single operation. The piece-rate shows that. But the cost of the labor turnover is an overhead cost that takes into account every relation of employer and employee. It can be ascertained only by the uncertain estimates of cost accounting. The scientific study of goodwill is, first of all, the accurate analysis of turnover and the apportionment of overhead costs to each element. When estimates vary as widely as they do at present, from $5.00 for common labor, to $400.00 for motormen, as the cost of losing a man and getting another fitted into his place, it is evident that the scientific study of goodwill is yet only in its theoretical stage. And it can never be other than an estimate of costs depending largely on the bias of the cost accountant. For, look at the many elusive items to be taken into account in estimating the overhead cost of labor turnover, such as cost of hiring, of training the new worker, of extra power, of lost profits, of fixed charges on plant while learning, of spoiled work, of extra wear and tear of machinery, of accidents to green employees, of loss of business on account of defective product, and so on.[1]

It is this unmeasured quality of goodwill that scientific managers are feeling after when they explain the breakdown of scientific management. Mr. Taylor explains it by saying that employers are too hasty for profits and are not willing to wait for the slow and patient work of science.[2] Mr. Hoxie points out that of the thirty or forty establishments picked out by scientific managers and recommended to him for investigation only two or three had carried out completely the patient trials, tests, experiments, upon which alone can science be called scientific.[3] Before time-and-motion studies are even begun with the workmen, two or three years may be needed to bring about the proper engineering revision of the physical plant. Not until that is accomplished is the truly scientific manager ready to enter the field of labor's habits, traditions, prejudices and old-fashioned ways of doing things.

Even then, the expert is only an adviser. He is an

[1] The most complete and critical study of the statistics is that recently made by Sumner Slichter in *The Turnover of Factory Labor*, Appleton, 1919.

[2] Taylor, *Principles of Scientific Management*, pp. 128–135.

[3] Hoxie, *Scientific Management and Labor*, p. 29.

outsider without authority. It is the employer who installs the devices and controls their use. So, scientific managers reach the point where they instruct, not the workman, but the employer. They urge him to give to the scientific man authority in his establishment. The employer should give up his desire for immediate profits and should abdicate in favor of the scientific engineer. The autocratic method breaks down at the point where profits without science take control of the worker.

It is this that stands in the way of any automatic solution of the labor problem that the engineer may devise. He can fashion a machine or lay out a factory and then go away and leave it to work according to its inherent forces. So he fixes up a scheme of nicely adjusted measurements and inducements by which he expects the human machine to turn out a product. Then he goes away and leaves it to the employer to operate, in confidence that he has invented an automatic solution of the labor problem.

This might suffice if he could tie up the worker by a contract that would hold him to work, no matter what changes subsequently occur. But the labor contract is not automatic and is not enforceable according to specifications. It is a new contract every day and every hour. It is the only contract that is not sacred. If, when a man is hired for a period of time, he could be compelled to fulfill his contract, the result would be involuntary servitude. On the other hand, if an employer is compelled to keep a man according to contract, then the employer might be compelled to have on his hands a man not suited to his work or not willing to work. So, in the last

forty years, since the Thirteenth Amendment to the
Constitution, the labor contract has become univer-
sally, except in the case of certain professional services,
a contract terminable at will without damages col-
lectible in court. The workman can be fired at any
hour of the day and he can quit at any hour, regardless of what promise has been made and without a
legal penalty. So the labor contract is new at every
turn of the work that is being done. The laborer is
bargaining while he is working, and his tacit offer
to the employer is the amount of work he is turning
out. If the employer accepts the offer he keeps him
at work. If the employer wants a different contract
the old one is already terminated by the very words
that suggest a change in the amount of work.

Scientific managers have sometimes tried to meet
this situation by stipulating that prices and premiums once set shall never be changed. But this is
impossible, and such a promise must be broken. Good
faith may possibly be kept with a certain individual
even though he may double and treble his wages
unexpectedly. Even that is unlikely. When he leaves
his job, when another takes his place, when unemployment breaks the connection, the moral obligation may
be deemed fulfilled. A new contract is made, a
different price is set. The individual promise may
not be violated but the contract changes with individuals. The promise made to one does not hold
with his successor, nor even with him if the job
changes.

Generally, instead of a promise that the price shall
never be changed the promise is made that it shall
hold for a year. This is about as far as the promise can

go. Even then, the daily work and wages are the tacit offers made in advance and in contemplation of their effect on the new bargain when it comes to be made. There must be a change sooner or later. Industry is improving, and if no change is made in the contract, the worker gets the sole benefit of progress at the expense of capital or the consumer. On the other hand, competition forces the employer to cut the rates or go out of business.

So, for these reasons, an automatic system designed as an ultimate solution to wind up the labor problem and let it work itself out is impossible. The labor problem is a daily trial of strength. The socialists call it a class struggle. It is a continuous bargain every day and hour, renewed either in the prices that are to be paid or the amount of product that the worker turns out. And it is this very renewal of bargains that constitutes goodwill in law and in fact.

Goodwill is the offspring of liberty and grows in importance as liberty enlarges. The slave-owner does not depend on goodwill, else he would emancipate his slaves. When the labor contract was enforced in law, the crime of running away was the employer's substitute for goodwill. And if the employer's competitors do not have access to his laborers, in order to give them information about alternative offers, it is not their goodwill that he depends upon, but their ignorance.

For goodwill is competitive persuasion. It is knowledge of alternatives and freedom to choose them without penalty or sacrifice. If there are no alternatives, or no knowledge of them, there is no goodwill. In prosperous times, when alternatives are numerous, the turnover increases. In hard times it is reduced. In prosperous times, too, the workers reduce their output. In hard times they work harder. And this is the curious paradox of modern industry and of the supply-and-demand theory of labor, that in hard times when there is already an overproduction of products relative to demand, the workers still further increase the overproduction by working harder; while in good times when demand outruns supply, the workers intensify the undersupply by still further reducing output. The manufacturer or merchant *reduces* his output when there is an oversupply on the market, but the wage-earner *increases* his, and *vice versa*. Commenting on this situation during a period of prosperity a great employer once said to me, "Yes, these fellows will not work now, but hard times will come and then we will soak them." With such a theory and such conditions it is fear rather than goodwill, retaliation rather than reciprocity, servility rather than freedom, that governs labor's production of wealth. Scientific management has made a great advance away from this commodity theory and its results. To the scientific study of goodwill and labor turnover we must look for a still greater advance.

For goodwill is coming to be an intangible asset of business more valuable than the tangible properties. It is the life of a going concern. Business goodwill, commercial goodwill, trade name, trade reputation, trade marks, often exceed in value the physical plant and the inventory of stock on hand. Goodwill is valuable because it lifts the business somewhat above the daily menace of competition and enables it to thrive without cutting prices. And what is "good credit" but the goodwill of bankers and investors?

So industrial goodwill is a valuable asset like commercial goodwill and good credit, and becomes so, more and more, in proportion as laborers acquire more liberty, power, intelligence and more inclination to assert their liberties. It too is valuable because it brings larger profits and lifts the employer somewhat above the level of competing employers by giving him a more productive labor force than theirs in proportion to the wages paid. And this larger profit reflects itself in the larger value of stocks and bonds, the higher capitalization of the going business. Goodwill is the expectation of future profit, and whether it be the commercial goodwill of patrons and customers, or the credit goodwill of bankers and investors, or the industrial goodwill of laborers, it has its present market value, sometimes greater than the value of all the tangible property of the business. Indeed, without goodwill, the tangible property is a liability rather than an asset.

But goodwill is fragile as well as intangible. It is not merely past reputation, it requires continuous upkeep through continuous repetition of service. It breaks down easily by deterioration, for it is built up on the most fragile of assets, the freedom of the will of patrons or workers. It cannot be wound up and allowed to run itself like a machine. It is not an exclusive monopoly protected by law like a patent right. It is not even a contract enforceable in law. It is just the intangible chance of making a contract if you can. It is menaced by competitors who are perhaps just as free and able as the owner to build up their own goodwill by making contracts, and only the employer who seriously appreciates the increasing importance of this aspect of the labor market will meet successfully either the counter-inducements of his competitors or the growing demands of the public that supports the cause of labor.

For it is goodwill that converts the "class struggle" of socialism into class harmony. It converts retaliation into reciprocity. Where it does not exist, there the public, more and more, is turning to another theory, not merely the goodwill theory of labor but the public-utility theory of labor.

IV

THE PUBLIC

Goodwill is a matter of public importance, for it builds up a harmony of interests, where both parties gain reciprocal advantage in comparison with competitors. The courts have long recognized this private advantage as also a public advantage, and finally Congress created the Federal Trade Commission in order to help eliminate unfair competition in the buying and selling of commodities, and thus protect commercial goodwill.

But fair competition does not eliminate free competition, and free competition may be cut-throat competition. There are always inefficient competitors and those who seek advantages by slashing prices. Their methods are not unfair as long as they do not get business away from any individual competitor by unfair methods directed against him individually. Cut-throat competition is directed against *all* competitors and brings down the general level of all prices or wages, since all competitors must meet it. Goodwill tells nothing of the general level. It tells only that one concern is making more profit than its competitors. Free competition tells where the general level shall be. Goodwill is an individual matter. Free competition affects the class of competitors as a whole.

It is for this reason that labor legislation comes in

to supplement goodwill. Competition tends to bring the advanced employers down to the level of the backward. It reduces the general level. Legislation forces the worst to come up toward the level of the more advanced and eliminates the backward. It raises the general level.

There always have been and always will be individual employers in advance of anything that legislation has done or can do. The first great employer of this kind was Robert Owen, one hundred years ago, who reduced the hours of labor in his cotton mills to ten per day and made a fortune when others were working their employees fifteen or sixteen hours.[1]

Today, when legislation in Wisconsin, for example, sets the limit of hours for women at 54 per week, a few leading employers adopt 49, and make more money, for they get and keep a higher grade of help. Always individual employers, for one reason or another, usually a combination of good business and public spirit, go ahead of legislation and set the example. Then legislation follows and attempts to force others to improve conditions, raise wages or shorten hours. The progressive ones cannot go far ahead of the general level, and they need not. On the other hand, legislation could, with difficulty, get popular or legal support if pioneers had not already shown that it wa practicable and profitable.

So legislation supplements goodwill and goodwill pioneers legislation. Goodwill is an individual matter. Legislation is class legislation. Goodwill raises the individual above his class. Legislation raises the class

[1] See Podmore, *Robert Owen, A Biography* (London, 1906), Vol. I p. 162.

as a whole. Goodwill does not reach the entire field. For those whom it does not reach, who do not care for the goodwill of labor, or who are unable, incompetent or unprogressive, the state comes in and tries to force them to do something nearly as good or to eliminate them entirely.

This may be called the public-utility theory of labor. If labor were simply a private affair it would be plainly unconstitutional under our principles of government to use the sovereign power to take something away from employers and hand it over to their employees. The public power cannot and should not be used for private purposes. But if the welfare of labor is a part of the public welfare, and if the piece of legislation in question is suited to the purpose in hand, then those who stand in the way are an injury to the public as well as to labor and may be restrained in the public interest.

To the anarchist or individualist there is no public purpose. Each individual is sovereign and has a natural right to do as he pleases. Private benefit is the only standard of action. To the socialist and syndicalist both the individual and the nation are illusions. There is simply one class struggling against another class, uncontrolled by any genuine ideas of patriotism, general welfare, or public utility. It is private war going on without a public purpose.

But in our constitutional democracy a private benefit or a class benefit may be a public benefit, depending on circumstances and public opinion. In the earlier days "the public" was looked upon as mainly composed of consumers, whose interest was best promoted by low prices and low wages of producers. Labor as such was not a part of the public. Slave labor was private property and the wages and hours of free labor were not matters of public consequence. Beginning with the protective tariff after 1840, American labor began to have national importance against the cheap labor of Europe. Public opinion had changed so that when the new tariffs came in, the purpose was no longer protection of capital but protection of labor.[1]

There were political, humanitarian and economic reasons for this change in opinion. Labor began to have the suffrage after the decade 1820. Labor suffered bitterly during the long depression following the panic of 1837. Labor began to have purchasing power, and high wages for home labor would improve the home market. Thus American labor was recognized as a part of the American nation so far as foreign nations were concerned.

But it required many years before labor was recognized as part of the public so far as American employers were concerned. Most of the legislation protecting them was declared unconstitutional, as being class legislation. While it was plainly a public purpose to protect labor against foreigners it was not such to protect them against their own employers.

This class of decisions prevailed until 1898 when the famous case of Holden v. Hardy was decided.[2] The legislatures of Utah and Colorado reduced the

---

[1] Mangold, George B., *The Labor Argument in the American Protective Tariff Discussion*, University of Wisconsin, *Bulletin* No. 246, Economics and Political Science Series, Vol. V, No. 2 (1908); Commons, *Labor and Administration*, Chapter XVIII, p. 350.

[2] Holden v. Hardy, 169 U. S. 366 (1898).

hours of labor in mines and smelters to eight per day. The Supreme Court of Colorado declared the law unconstitutional. The Supreme Court of Utah declared it constitutional. The Supreme Court of the United States supported the Utah court. Prior to that time the health of consumers was, of course, recognized as a public purpose. By that decision it came to be recognized that workers also were a part of the public, and legislation on behalf of their health while at work would not be class legislation but reasonable classification for a public purpose. A benefit to the workers became a benefit to the public.

The court also advanced the proposition that instead of the employer and employee being equal they were unequal in power. Up to that time the court's notion of equality assumed that the employer and the employee were equal and had equal power. It had previously been held that in the case of children and women there was inequality. Children and women could constitutionally be protected, for they were weak in bargaining power and could not protect themselves against the employer. Now the court held that men also were weaker than employers in bargaining power.

If a class is not able to protect itself against another class and if there is a public purpose involved, then class legislation becomes reasonable classification. The court would not have sustained an eight-hour law applying to all labor of all classes, but it sustained a law applying to labor where it was being injured, under harsh conditions. The court rendered a different decision in the baker's case from New York. There the legislature tried to limit the hours of labor to 10 per day for bakers. The court said in effect that there was no public purpose involved, and that there was no inequality in bargaining power. The legislation was class legislation, for it attempted to benefit one class at the expense of another.[1]

So the court's opinion has differed for different classes of labor according to conditions and according to the court's idea of whether there is a public purpose involved. Labor is not a part of the public unless it is recognized as having a public importance. The state or nation cannot legislate for a class of persons if they are merely private persons and the benefit is merely a private benefit.

But in the historical development of legislation, people who have not been a part of the public finally become a part by being admitted into citizenship and granted certain rights of public protection by imposing corresponding duties on other citizens. Prior to that they are treated as commodities to be bought and sold according to supply and demand. Afterward they are treated as citizens with rights against others on account of their value to the nation as a whole.

What are the qualities in a person which constitute that person a part of the public? The first quality is health. That probably is the most fundamental public purpose. If a certain class is part of the public, then the health of that class is important. The health of that class becomes a public utility.

Next come morality and character. While our government protects property, yet if property is deemed to interfere with morals our courts are more

[1] Lochner v. New York, 198 U. S. 45 (1905).
3

destructive than those of other nations. Other nations perhaps would not permit prohibition of the liquor traffic without compensation to the distillers and brewers. In this country, when public opinion gets to the point where it considers a thing immoral, our courts refuse to protect that property at all and the value of the property can be destroyed without compensation. England, when she freed her slaves, compensated the owners. In this country that was not done.

Coercion and oppression are also public disadvantages. In the Holden v. Hardy case it was recognized that inequality o bargaining power was a public disadvantage, that the state is concerned in having equal powers among individuals. Where they are unequal, if a public purpose is served thereby, the employers may be deprived, without compensation, of their greater liberty, power and property rights.

Who is it that decides these questions? Who decides whether labor is a public utility or not? Who is it that decides what qualities are of public importance? In this country it is the voters. We call their decision public opinion. We say that public opinion decides. But the Supreme Court can veto public opinion or have a different view from that of the voters and can place its opinion against the voter's opinion. So we have judicial opinion as well as public opinion. If the Supreme Court approves of what the voters decide, it is constitutional. If it d es not approve, then it is unconstitutional. The court can change its opinion and it does change its opinion, just as the voters change theirs.

What are the conditions that bring about this

change of opinion, both judicial and public? First is the development of economic conditions. Health, morals, welfare, liberty, power, equality, are all changed by the changes brought about by modern industry. Second, labor is a moving force and an important force in maintaining and operating this economic machinery. Formerly it was not considered so important. Now, more and more, we see that labor is quite as important as the employer. Third, is the growth in notions of ethics and justice. The humanitarian notions which began in the decade of the thirties of the past century have changed both public and judicial opinion. Fourth, scientific investigation, knowledge of these conditions, is more accurate. We have had very little scientific investigation of labor until the past twenty years. The earliest investigations of health of working people were made about 1838–1840. They dealt with the effect of factory conditions on working women and children. Prior to these investigations public opinion might be merely prejudiced; now it becomes scientific and informed. There can be no substantial or safe progress without scientific investigation. There may be revolution and reaction, but not progress.

But the constitutional method is based on ascertained facts and goes ahead and stays. It is this that constitutes "due process of law." It is this that marks the decisions of the court since the case of Holden v. Hardy. Since then, the economic and sociological briefs of Mr. Louis Brandeis and others have laid before the Supreme Court of the United States the opinions and investigations of medical people, of boards of health, of factory inspectors and all classes of experts on labor's condition. It is these that have begun to enlighten the court, and in proportion as courts and other lawyers adapt in this way their legal precedents to the new conditions does the public purpose of labor legislation get recognized and that which was class legislation becomes reasonable protection of labor in the interest of the nation.[1]

[1] Commons and Andrews, *Principles of Labor Legislation*, pp. 422–430.

V

DEMOCRACY

Two extreme ideas of democracy gained temporary triumph during the two great revolutions at the end of the eighteenth and the beginning of the twentieth centuries.

The French Revolution brought in the anarchistic idea of democracy. Every individual was to be absolutely free to do as he pleased. Not only were all privileges of nobility, church and monarchy abolished, but all corporations, all associations or gilds, all employers' associations or trade unions, that tied the individual down by the vote of his association, were prohibited.[1] It was believed that individuals were equal by nature, and if so, the self-interest of each, if not interfered with by government or by associations whose by-laws the government enforced, would work out harmoniously for the good of all. The anarchistic idea of democracy is equal liberty for every individual, but not for any associations of individuals.

We know how this theory of democracy has worked. If allowed to go on, it ends in the despotism of powerful individuals. People are neither equal nor unselfish. Government has necessarily come in to restrain powerful and unscrupulous individuals and classes, and pro-

[1] See Dicey, *Law and Opinion in England*, Appendix, Note I, pp. 467–476.

tect the weak and scrupulous. Besides, individuals seldom act as individuals. They act as associations.

The Russian Revolution, on the other hand, culminated in the socialistic idea of democracy. Labor produces all wealth and is entitled to the whole product. But the individual laborer is powerless to get that product. So, organized labor takes possession of the factories. The owners are disfranchised and the labor unions operate both the government and the industries.[1] The socialistic idea of democracy means the dictatorship of organized labor.

We have seen how this theory works. The sovyets could not get business ability or managing ability to come in and direct their factories because they had wiped out profits; and they could not get new capital to come in because they had ruined credit.

The anarchistic idea of democracy is based on the hope that individuals will voluntarily be brothers and live in harmony if they are not coerced by laws that enforce the rights of property. The socialistic idea of democracy is based on the hope that class struggle will stop when the only class that governs is the labor class.

But even brothers do not always live in harmony, and class struggle never will stop. As long as nature's resources are limited in supply, as long as labor, science, capital, and management are needed to increase the supply of products, as long as the demand for food, clothing, shelter and other services is greater than the supply, so long will there be disharmony and opposition of interests. At one end is consumption of wealth which always wants more of it. At the other

---

[1] See Ross, *Russia in Upheaval*, p. 208 *ff*.

end is production of wealth which always means sacrifice and effort. As long as resources are limited and wants unlimited there will be struggle between individuals and classes.

The struggle is permanent and irrepressible, but may be, and is, reconciled more or less as we go along. We cannot wait for the millenium either of anarchism or socialism, for it assumes both perfectibility of human nature and unlimited supply of products. That means the life beyond. The war has forced us to adopt ideas of democracy suited to this imperfect world.

After Congress and the President had authorized Mr. Hoover to fix the price of wheat, he looked around for somebody who could represent the producers of wheat and somebody who could represent the consumers of flour. He found certain farmer's organizations that could be said to speak for the farmers. He found that the body that came nearest to representing the consumers was the American Federation of Labor. He asked these organizations to appoint representatives to assist him, which they did. He had also his own experts and statisticians. The farmers wanted $2.50 per bushel. The laborers thought $1.84 was enough. Mr. Hoover wanted the wheat in large quantities. After several days they compromised on $2.20.

This was representative democracy in industry. It was class struggle reconciled in the public interest. Mr. Hoover did not fix the price of wheat. President Wilson did not fix the price. It was fixed by organized labor and organized agriculture. Afterward an effort was made in Congress to go over this price and place it at $2.50 in the alleged interest of the farmers. It would have been just as reasonable for the laborers to have violated the compromise and for Congress to have put the price at $1.84 in the alleged interest of the laborers.

Congress does not directly represent either farmers or consumers. It may be political democracy, but it is not industrial democracy. Representative democracy in industry is representation of organized interests.[1] Individuals who are not organized cannot choose representatives. They must content themselves with their tacit proxies given to the organized. When once organized they can be consulted in advance of action. The procedure of autocracy is to act first and consult afterwards. The procedure of democracy is to consult first and act afterwards.

But democracy cannot quickly consult all individuals whose interests are affected. It comes as near as possible to doing it when it consults those who have been freely chosen for the purpose without interference from other classes, so that they really represent the individuals of the class affected. No man who is "disinterested" can represent opposing interests. But when the interested man is consulted, then the interests that select him are substantially consulted. When he agrees, then those with similar interests have agreed.

For Congress to have fixed the price of wheat at $2.50 would have been as autocratic as for an oligarchy of farmers to have fixed it at that price. For Congress to have fixed it at $1.84 would have been

---

[1] See Commons, *Labor and Administration*, p. 55 *ff*; *Proportional Representation*, pp. 355–363.

to submit to the "dictatorship of the proletariat." For Mr. Hoover and his staff to have fixed the price would have been government by "bureaucracy." For the organized interests to fix it themselves under expert advice of the nation's food administrator and his statisticians was the practical democratic way of doing it. It was the procedure of appealing to the harmony of interest of both classes for the public good.

Again, the attempt was made for nearly a year to bring together employers and employees for production of munitions of war, under the direction of a trade unionist as Secretary of Labor. Notwithstanding his great ability and unquestioned fairness it was impossible to secure the coöperation of employers. He represented but one of the opposing interests, and his staff lacked the business experience and record of impartiality needed to obtain their confidence. Finally, the President directed the Secretary of Labor to select as his advisers representative employers and employees. He went to the one great organization of employers, the National Industrial Conference Board, and to the great organization of employees, the American Federation of Labor. Each side appointed five representatives and they in turn each selected the most representative professional men in the country, ex-President Taft, to lead the employers, and Frank P. Walsh to lead the workingmen.

Forthwith this representative body formulated a national labor program, which the Secretary adopted, "to maintain maximum production by settling obstructive controversies between employers and workers."[1]

Somewhat similar arrangements were made to cover

---

[1] *Official Bulletin*, April 1, 1918, p. 7.

all of the vital activities of the Department, including employment offices, housing, etc. With this staff of investigators, adjustors, and executives, having the confidence of all parties, a further step in advance was made in bringing about the union of efficiency and democracy.[1]

Other departments of war administration illustrate the same principle. The Fuel Administration had its leading coal operators and the President of the United Mine Workers of America. The Shipping Board, the War Industries Board, and others, to a greater or less degree, formally or informally, followed the same procedure.

So, in the stress of national peril American democracy called to its aid, not only distinguished individuals, but the organized opposing class interests of the nation. The organizations themselves were incorporated in the framework of government. No longer were they merely private associations carrying on private contests, distrusted and even outlawed, but they were raised to the level of recognized public importance. Organized labor, organized farmers, organized capitalists became public utilities.

Democracy takes on a new meaning, the partnership of classes. Like any partnership they have their disputes. In times of peace or in non-essential industries, these may be matters of public indifference. They are private affairs. In time of national peril, or in strategic industries, they are vital to national

[1] *Official Bulletin*, January 16, 1918, p. 8; April 1, 1918, p. 1; May 14, 1918, p. 1; Wehle, Louis B., "Labor Problems in the United States During the War," *Quarterly Journal of Economics*, February, 1918; Marshall, L. C., "The War Labor Program and Its Administration," *Journal of Political Economy*, May, 1918.

security or prosperity. The organizations themselves perform public functions. The nation cannot live without enlisting them.

Over and above the individuals composing them, they become a more embracing public utility. Only through organization can the modern industrial worker, whether capitalist or laborer, have an effective voice either in industry or government. His liberty is bound to be limited anyhow by the liberties and powers of opponents or competitors. In his individual weakness he gains greater power and liberty through organization. And representative democracy is neither the imagined anarchistic equality of individuals nor the socialistic dictatorship of labor, but it is the equilibrium of capital and labor—the class partnership of organized capital and organized labor, in the public interest.

The thing may not be always easy in practice. It may not always work smoothly. Strikes and struggles may come. But "the public" cannot listen to any proposal to suppress either kind of organization. If one is suppressed then the other becomes dictator. The equilibrium of democracy may not be easy to work out, but what else is there to do? Even if suppression is attempted it cannot for long succeed. The first national crisis sets the suppressor aside. President Wilson, who in times past had criticized restrictive practices of unions, yet, when the crisis came, attended the national convention of organized labor and pledged the nation's support to their proper demands.[1]

[1] *War, Labor and Peace*, Number 9, Red, White and Blue Series, Issued by the Committee on Public Information, p. 7. An address before the Convention of the American Federation of Labor, held in Buffalo, New York.

And ex-President Taft, whose judicial decisions had set up standards of government injunctions obstructive to unionism, when he became responsible for the labor policy of the war, notified the Western Union Telegraph Company that the truce between capital and labor did not include the maintenance of the "closed non-union shop."[1] In the national peril, the policy of both the President and the ex-President goes beyond their earlier opinions as professor or judge, and throws the weight of the nation on the side of encouraging unions to go out and organize the unorganized. Organization is bound to come, in one form or another, under the stress of economic conditions. Rather than leave it to the anarchistic or socialistic unions that propose both to take over the employer's property and to break down the patriotism of labor, they place the nation's trust in the unions which through their representatives had agreed with the employers to support the industries of the nation. Such a union serves indeed a public purpose, and no one is in a better position to know it than he upon whom, like President Wilson or ex-President Taft, is laid the chief responsibility of carrying the nation through its crisis.

At the very time when these momentous decisions were being made by executive departments of government, the judicial department handed down a majority decision holding, in effect, that a union is a mere private affair and therefore has no right, against the employer's wish, to go among his employees and even persuade them to join the union.[2] The corporation,

[1] *Official Bulletin*, June 4, 1918, p. 6.
[2] Hitchman Coal and Coke Company v. John Mitchell et al., 245 U. S. 229 (1917).

said the majority of the court, "is entitled to the goodwill of its employees, precisely as a merchant is entitled to the goodwill of his customers, although they are under no obligation to continue to deal with him."

Prior to this decision the similar cases went off on the allegation of coercion or intimidation. In this case the decision went to the final limit of prohibiting even persuasion by the agents of a labor union. Even the "goodwill" theory was distorted, for goodwill is competitive persuasion, and this the court attempts to prohibit, if the competitor is a labor union.

Two opposing rights were in conflict, the right of the corporation and the right of the trade union. If both are merely private associations then the right of the corporation prevails. It had cemented its rights by oral contracts with its workmen in which they agreed to work as non-union men. If there is no public purpose opposed to such contracts, then even persuasion by labor organizations is an illegal conspiracy.

The dissenting opinion of the minority of the court maintained that the efforts of the union to persuade employees were not illegal since the contracts with their employers were not like other contracts but were terminable at will. Neither was the "closed union shop" policy of the union coercive any more than the "closed non-union shop" policy of the corporation. Both policies being therefore persuasive and not coercive, the persuasion offered to join the union was legal, provided the purpose of the union was justifiable. That purpose was "confessedly in order to strengthen the union, in the belief that thereby the condition of

workmen engaged in mining would be improved;
the bargaining power of the individual workingman
was to be strengthened by collective bargaining."[1]

Is such a purpose legal or illegal? The majority
held that it was illegal when it interfered with the
employer's goodwill and labor contracts. The minority held that it was legal. "It should not," said the
minority opinion, "at this day be doubted that to
induce workingmen to leave or not to enter an
employment in order to advance such a purpose, is
justifiable when the workmen are not bound by contract to remain in such employment."

Thus, in the final analysis, the legality or illegality
of a labor union turns on the opinion of the judge or
the executive or the public as to the public purpose
of the union. If it exists only for a private purpose,
then even its persuasive efforts are illegal. If it
performs a public purpose, then its effort to strengthen
its bargaining power by persuasion is lawful. All
other details and all technical reasoning of the law are
subordinate to this.

Does it, or does it not, serve a public purpose?
Each person must decide for himself. When he
decides, we know his definition of democracy. If
the union performs no public purpose then democracy
is the anarchistic, socialistic or capitalistic definition
of democracy, and only those who have the power may
govern if they wish. But if both associations of
workmen and associations of employers perform a
public service, then neither can be left to dominate

[1] Hitchman Coal and Coke Company v. John Mitchell et al., 245
U. S. 229, 273 (1917).

the other, but both unite in a representative democracy as the means of promoting the public welfare.

For, the struggle of capital and labor is almost never a struggle of individuals. It always involves associations of individuals. The court starts with a fiction that a corporation is a "person" and then holds that an individual worker and an individual corporation are exactly equal, in that the right of one person to quit work is exactly equal to the right of the other person to discharge him. It thereupon declares unconstitutional all the laws in which the legislature tries to protect, against employers, the worker's right to belong to a union, by prohibiting employers from discharging them solely on account of union membership.[1]

These decisions are absurd enough in the case of a corporation, which is obviously an association of capitalists. The right of a worker to quit working for an association of capitalists is by no means equal to the right of the association of capitalists to discharge him.

The legal decisions are equally absurd in the case of a so-called "individual" employer. Every employer, whether incorporated or not, is an association of capitalists, for he is an association of all the bankers, investors, creditors, material men, who have trusted their capital to him. He speaks as one man for his association of capitalists.

And the courts have worked out, on behalf of associated capital, an elaborate and highly perfected law of "principal and agent." When a foreman,

[1] Adair v. U. S. 208 U. S. 161 (1908); Coppage v. Kansas 236 U. S. 1 (1915); Cf. Freund, *Standards of American Legislation*, pp. 225–248.

or superintendent, or manager, fires an employee
or threatens to fire him, or refuses to deal with him,
he is the agent who concentrates on that man the
combined power of all the capitalists, investors,
and creditors connected with the business.   The claim
of laborers to have the right to organize is simply their
claim to come under this law of principal and agent.
The right of labor to organize is but the right of
laborers to speak as one man through one agent
for their association of laborers.   The employer
always speaks as a representative of associated capital.
Unless the laborer can speak as a representative of
associated laborers, he cannot speak with equal power.
Neither the nation nor the laborers can remain
content until the Supreme Court reverses these
decisions[1] and falls in line with effective democracy.
For, effective democracy is representative democracy.

[1] Adair v. U. S. 208 U. S. 161 (1908); Coppage v. Kansas 236 U. S.
1 (1915); Hitchman Coal and Coke Company v. John Mitchell et al.,
245 U. S. 229 (1917).

VI

SOLIDARITY

Under the workmen's compensation law, a case in dispute came before the Industrial Commission of Wisconsin for decision. A teamster got drunk on his employer's time, fell off his wagon and was killed. His widow petitioned for the award of indemnity to be paid by the employer. The law provided that no compensation should be paid in cases of "willful misconduct."

Evidently, from one point of view, it was his own willful misconduct that caused the teamster's death. He had even driven out of his way and taken an hour of his employer's time to go to the saloon and buy the whiskey that killed him. From the standpoint of individual responsibility for that particular accident, the worker alone was responsible and it would be a flagrant injustice to require the employer to pay $2000 to the widow and orphans on account of an accident for which the employer was not responsible. So reasoned the employer and such were the precepts of the common law which make each individual responsible for his own acts and not for the acts of other persons.

But the workmen's compensation law had abolished the employer's defense of contributory negligence, except where the contributory negligence was the "willful misconduct" of the employee. The Commission had to decide whether drunkenness was willful misconduct. If it was, then the widow and orphans had to suffer the cost of the accident. If it was not, then the employer had to pay them about $2000 toward tiding them over the period of poverty and infancy.

The Commission, after much hesitation, decided in favor of the widow and orphans. It was not willful misconduct. The drunken man did not intend to kill himself. They decided that by "willful misconduct" was meant an injury intentionally self-inflicted.

The Commission, perhaps, weighed the consequences of willful misconduct rather than the accepted meaning of the term. Somebody must pay the cost of accidents. Shall it be the widows and orphans themselves? Shall it be the tax-payers and the charities? Shall it be the individual employer? Shall it be the industry as a whole? Somebody must decide. Formerly the widows and orphans paid when the breadwinner was at fault; then the charities; then the tax-payers. The Commission figured that the lawmakers intended that the industry should pay the first cost of accidents. The Supreme Court sustained the decision.[1] Afterward similar cases arose. A sailor fell overboard while drunk and the employer was required to pay compensation to his widow and orphans On the former legal theory of individual responsibility these decisions could not be justified.

[1] Nekoosa-Edwards Paper Co. v. Mittie Smith, 154 Wis. 105 (1913). The legislature afterward sustained the opinion and made the law explicit by substituting "intentionally self-inflicted" for "willful misconduct."

Only on a theory of partnership or solidarity of interest can they find justification.

Employer and employee are engaged in a common enterprise. They jointly assume the risks and share the burdens and benefits of the enterprise.

More than that. They share each other's frailties. The employer takes the workman as he is, and the workman takes the employer as he is. The employer gains in some cases and loses in other cases, and the law attempts to balance one off against the other. The employer *gains* in those cases where he alone is responsible, for, instead of heavy damages of many thousand dollars where a man is badly disabled through the employer's fault, he pays only a moderate compensation previously set forth in the statute. The employer *loses* where the worker is responsible, for he pays the same compensation as when he himself is responsible.

The law attempts to set off the frailties of one against the frailties of the other, and to balance off the chances of human nature with its imperfections as they are. Each takes the other as he is, with all his frailties.

Each also takes the occupation as it exists, with all its risks. They engage jointly in a common enterprise. The risks of the enterprise and the risks of each other are shared by each according to a schedule of prices set forth in advance. If the sailor did not go to sea he would not drown even if drunk, nor even if his employer were criminally careless. If the employer did not own vessels and hire sailors to operate them he would not run the risk of drowning drunk sailors. It requires the risks of the business, the risks of human nature and the partnership of capital and labor to produce industrial accidents.

Partnership is an economic fact. It may or may not be recognized. But if it is a fact it will ultimately force us to recognize it and give it a place in our theories. It is a fact forced upon us by the way in which business is carried on, and by the alternatives that would happen if we did not accept it. Without even knowing what we do we are compelled to act sometimes according to those consequences. The theory comes afterward and helps us to explain our own acts. The Industrial Commission, as practical men, acted perhaps in view of consequences and their idea of the purpose of the law. Eventually the theory of solidarity is formulated and serves to justify similar acts.

The employer who has not yet accepted the theory of solidarity has a wrong attitude toward the law. He contests the cases where he is not at fault. He is litigious and incensed at the injustice of paying damages due to the frailties of others. He cultivates ill-will.

Probably 10 per cent of accidents are owing to infection of trivial wounds. Infection would not follow an accident if the worker had resorted to the employer's "first aid." Infection is due to the worker's misconduct. Yet the employer takes the worker as he is and pays the damages of infection. Hernia, epilepsy, and other frailties, are often inherited predispositions. Without inherited or acquired weaknesses many of the accidents in industry would not occur. Yet the industry pays the cost of the worker's defects just as it pays the costs of defects in machinery.

What are the consequences of accepting the theory of solidarity?

A safety engineer showed his general manager that the time lost on account of accidents would have turned out 35 more automobiles that year. Safety work had been classed as unproductive labor. What the worker suffers from accidents is self-evident. What the employer suffered was not so plain. Accident prevention had been considered humanitarian. When it came to be seen that it produced profits as well as safety, then it entered the field of good business. For goodwill benefits both parties, and safety work is productive, for it builds up the goodwill of labor.

Because good business did not reach all employers, the several states began to supplement it by legislation. The public interest in accidents has arisen through new conditions and motives, well known, such as the new dangers of modern machinery and transportation, the fire hazard where labor is massed in factories, the recognition that labor is a part of the public, and the labor vote.

Legislation at first was repressive. The employer was treated as a criminal. New misdemeanors were created by law. Employers were ordered to safeguard machinery. The state appointed special police, the factory inspectors, to go about and discover if employers had obeyed the law by installing the safeguards. Evidence was collected and prosecution was started in court. The court presumes every man to be innocent unless proven guilty and gives him the benefit of every doubt. If the legislature failed to specify a certain point of danger, then there was no misdemeanor in leaving it dangerous. Thus the criminal theory of individual responsibility broke down.

But there was also the common-law theory of responsibility for injury. Every person must enjoy his own property in such a way as not to injure others. If, by his own acts, he invades the rights of others, he is liable in a suit for damages. But he is not responsible for the acts of third parties. So, in a suit for damages by an injured employee, the law allowed the employer to set up the defense that he was not responsible, by showing that someone else was responsible or had assumed responsibility. Perhaps the employee himself was careless, or he had assumed the risks of the occupation by the act of accepting the job, or a fellow-servant was responsible and should have been the one sued for damages. The common-law theory of individual responsibility broke down.

Meanwhile there had been growing up voluntarily a theory of group responsibility. Employers insured each other against the risks of accidents by paying premiums into a common fund which then could be drawn upon to meet the individual obligation of any subscriber in case of accident. Voluntarily employers assumed jointly each other's risks by taking out insurance with casualty companies. Voluntarily they acted on a theory of group responsibility.

But they insured themselves against the wrong thing. They insured themselves against the legal risk of a law suit and not against the industrial risk of injury to the worker. Further, they introduced a third party, the insurance company, between themselves and their workers. They agreed not to negotiate with their own employees in case of accident compensation, but to abandon the worker to a third party at the very moment when they ought to have devoted themselves most sympathetically to his welfare. Under such a system goodwill was impossible.

This impossible situation could be remedied only by compulsory compensation and compulsory insurance.

The common-law doctrine of individual responsibility was therefore revised, and the employer was made responsible for *all* accidents, whether they happened by his own fault, or the fault of a fellow-servant, or the contributory fault of the injured workman himself, or by nobody's fault.

Naturally, at first, the courts were inclined to look upon such a revolutionary law as unconstitutional. It deprived the employer of rights of property by compelling him to pay damages when he was not responsible for injury. The Supreme Court of New York declared that the workman's compensation law was unconstitutional, because that court held to the theory of individual responsibility. The statute deprived the employer of his property without due process of law, because it made him pay damages in cases where he was not at fault.[1] Afterward the constitution of the state was amended and the court then accepted the notion of solidarity.

The Supreme Court of the state of Washington took the opposite view. Employers as a class are made responsible for accidents to laborers as a class and can be required to contribute to a common insurance fund, so that the employer who has no accidents pays for the accidents in the shops of his

[1] Ives v. South Buffalo R. Co. 201 N. Y. 271 (1911).

competitors.[1] Partnership of capital and labor, solidarity of individuals within a class, group responsibility of employers, becomes a theory of jurisprudence to a limited extent, in place of the theory of individual responsibility.[2]

Statistics showed that accidents accompany industry as a whole, at different rates in different industries. The individual disappears in the statistical average. These accidents are a cost of production which must be met, like the breakage of machinery. Industry as a whole must bear the expense. Insofar as the expense is laid upon the laborer it can go no further. The common-law theory of demand and supply assumed that the laborer could shift the cost of the risks of the occupation upon the employer by demanding and getting higher wages. This was doubtful. At any rate, the individual laborer who met with the accident could not shift the cost of that particular accident. He is the ultimate producer and must endure the ultimate cost. But insofar as the cost can be laid upon the employer he is in a position to shift it to the ultimate consumer, by charging higher prices for the product. He is the worker's partner, agent and representative, selling the worker's product to the public. If the public is willing to share a part of the laborer's cost of accidents then the employer is the middleman to collect the bill and pay it back to the laborer.

Provided, however, that *all* employers are compelled to bear the same expense. If the indifferent,

[1] David Smith Co. v. Clausen, 65 Wash. 156 (1911).
[2] Cf. Freund, *Standards of American Legislation*, pp. 109–112; Gide and Rist, *A History of Economic Doctrines*, pp. 606, 607.

or incompetent, or inhuman employer can escape the expense, then his cut-throat competition prevents the others from shifting it by charging higher prices. The class responsibility of employers is the responsibility that the poorest or worst employer owes to the better employer not to force him down by competition to his lower level. Where he does not willingly meet this responsibility, legislation compels him to do it.

Compulsory compensation for accidents compels the careless, thoughtless, and inhuman employer to perform the same service for labor that the careful, competent or humane is already doing or wants to do. It raises the level of competition at that point, eliminates cut-throat competition, enforces the duty of fair competition, and shifts the cost to the consumer.

Compulsory insurance is the opposite of compulsory compensation. It compels the careful, competent, or humane employer to help pay for the accidents occurring in the shops of his careless competitors. When this is done voluntarily by an insurance contract, the employer's property, of course, is not taken except with his previous approval. When done by law it is taken without his consent. The details are immaterial. Whether it be done by insuring with a certified private insurance company, or by organizing an employer's mutual, or by paying into a state fund, or even by the self-insurance of a large corporation, all are alike in compelling contributions to a common fund adequate to pay the worker promptly when the accident happens.

Thus class legislation which imposes group responsibility works in two ways: it compels the backward employer to come up alongside the forward employer, and compels the forward employer to help along the backward one.

In this way, it recognizes what the socialists have called the "class struggle." The employers as a class are recognized as having a common interest immediately in opposition to the interests of the laborers as a class. But it recognizes it only in order to recognize the larger notion of solidarity. Instead of refusing to see and acknowledge the opposition of class interests where it really exists, as was the case when it was held that only the individual was responsible, it recognizes class antagonism by enforcing partnership and group responsibility. And, instead of the socialistic idea of eliminating class struggle by eliminating employers altogether and making organized labor the sovereign, it eliminates it by making employers responsible as a class to laborers as a class.

In doing so it makes them responsible for harmonizing the struggle between capital and labor. And it does so at the point where the class struggle was most bitter and humiliating—bitter because laborers felt that employers were grinding profit out of their flesh and blood; humiliating because employers, under the pressure of competition, were not free to safeguard and compensate their workers as they knew they should.

Thus compulsory compensation, with compulsory insurance, enlarges liberty more than it restrains it. It enlarges it in a different direction. It opens up a new field for initiative, individuality, enterprise and even profit. Instead of abolishing profit, as the socialists would do, it increases profits for the more competent. I know a corporation that had been paying about $5000 a year for insurance unde the old employer's liability law, when it paid for only a *small part* of the accidents. After the compensation law had been in effect a year or so it was paying only about $2000 a year, although it was paying for *all* of the accidents. It had simply prevented accidents. To reduce accidents 70 per cent is not unusual under this new inducement of more profit. Progressive employers go far ahead of what had ever been thought possible and far ahead of what the state could compel them to do by treating them as criminals. This class of legislation is not paternalistic or coercive but stimulating and persuasive.

Not only that, it leads the employer to educate his workmen in safety. Mechanical safeguarding can accomplish comparatively little. It is the "spirit" of safety in the workmen that accomplishes most. Industry is started toward representative democracy, for, in order to inspire the workmen with the spirit of safety, their coöperation must be won by taking their best representatives into a partnership of accident prevention through safety committees and safety organization of the shop.

And this goes beyond the shop, into the home. The National Safety Council, composed of the safety men of the great corporations, educates the entire nation in the spirit of safety.[1] A new profession is started. The claim agent, who used to follow up the injured workman promptly after an accident, in order to build up his employer's defenses against a damage

[1] See *Proceedings of the National Safety Council*, Chicago, beginning 1912.

suit, becomes the safety expert and the safety booster, coöperating with all the workers to benefit both them and their employer. Civil and mechanical engineers enlist. All of the high ideals of a profession, all the missionary zeal of the enthusiast, all the satisfaction of a noble work that saves life and health, now animate the members of this profession. They perform a public service while they bring together the employer and his hundreds of workers in the mutual benefits of goodwill. As a profession, they become independent. They lay down the law of safety and goodwill even to their employer, just as the lawyer or the accountant or the engineer tells him how to conduct his business within their professional fields.

And government itself takes on a new spirit. It ceases to be mainly repressive and becomes educational. A new type of factory inspector comes in, whose inspiring purpose it is to show the employer how to prevent accidents, rather than persecute him. And employers coöperate with government instead of resisting it. They hire their own safety inspectors and do their own inspecting, more efficiently than government police and courts ever could do it.

The final result is, instead of shifting the cost of compensation for accidents upon the ultimate consumer, through increased prices for products, there is no increased cost to be shifted. The laborer, indeed, continues to pay a large share of the cost of whatever accidents remain unprevented, for no compensation, however great, can fully compensate for loss of life or limb; but the share of cost that is thrown upon the employer becomes no cost but a source of profit. The consumer gains, the laborer gains, the employer gains, and that which started out to compel compensation to the laborer for his loss of time and his expense of medical care, turns out to have been the greatest of all instruments yet invented for preventing accidents. It enlists for that purpose a powerful motive that reaches even the remotest stock-holder who never sees the worker—the expectation of larger profits through initiative, enterprise, and good business. .The solidarity of capital and labor becomes the prosperity of capital, of labor, and the nation.

VII

THEORY AND PRACTICE

I have mentioned certain possible theories of labor. There are others. They are not facts, but theories. They are assumptions, hypotheses, philosophies, "principles," so-called, which are employed consciously or unconsciously, to explain the facts, or to guide in hunting facts, or to weigh the facts, or to decide what to do in view of the facts.

Everybody acts more or less on one or more of these theories or sets of principles. Practical people sometimes pride themselves that they deal with facts and not theories. "Two and two are four." It looks like a fact. But it is only a theory. It is not true unless it fits the facts. Two chairs and two beds are not four windows. Two dogs and two cats are not always four friends. The theory of "two and two are four" fits some facts and not others. It depends on the facts. It is an hypothesis, a guess, an assumption, a "principle." It is empty until it has been filled with facts, and then it takes good judgment to fill it with facts that fit.

One theory or set of principles may be true up to a certain point, where it comes in conflict with an inconsistent theory. Then that different theory must be introduced. The commodity theory explains some facts about labor, and is a good enough guess up to a certain point. The machinery theory is another that is satisfactory as far as it fits the facts. Goodwill is a different theory that may or may not be accepted according to our opinions regarding the facts and our wishes as to what we intend to do with the facts. The public-utility theory supplements the others, and our theories of democracy, of partnership, of solidarity, tell us what we will do with certain facts when they come up.

People differ among themselves mainly because they give different weights to different theories. The fanatic, or crank, or mere "theorist," is brother to the autocrat—he takes only one theory and rides it through to the death penalty. Such is also the practical man who insists that two and two are *always* four, and doesn't stop to ask, two and two *what?* Such people may become dangerous and then the people with different theories begin to close in on them. And the man who rides the commodity theory or the machinery theory to the limit is probably just as dangerous as the one who rides the anarchist theory or the socialist theory or the theory of democracy or partnership or solidarity to the limit.

The problem of industrial goodwill is really the problem of finding out how far the different theories are true and necessary at a given time and place, under given circumstances and given facts, in order to guide our acts, to hunt for hidden facts, to weigh the facts when found, and to get something that will work reasonably. The man who claims that he deals with facts and not with theories is usually one who is simply riding his own theory and calling it a fact. He thinks that two and two are always four because he has emptied the theory of facts, or because he has got accustomed to using the theory only where it fits certain facts, or because he is in the habit of picking out only that small portion of all the facts that fits his wishes or theory. The sane man is the man of common sense, who is willing to act on different theories, or rather on all the theories, and is willing to investigate and give due weight to all of the facts in the light of all the theories. Such a man is what is known in law as "reasonable."

VIII

SECURITY

If the commodity theory of labor is assumed, consciously or unconsciously, then wages are left to supply and demand. If the engineering theory is added, then the individual laborer is made more productive by the scientific study of him and his job. When the goodwill theory is adopted, we find the beginnings of serious attention to irregularity of employment. The labor turnover is an angle of the modern insecurity of labor that has come along with liberty. If industry is irregular and uncertain, then a man must be laid off and taken on again and the number of men hired and fired is increased. But if an establishment can give steady employment it can attract and hold workmen as against other employers whose work is irregular. To regularize employment is the first step in industrial goodwill.

For, of course, it is not a man's daily wages that fix his welfare, but it is his earnings over a period of time. A carpenter at $4.00 a day, 200 days a year, earns no more than another at $2.70 a day for 300 days. The high wages in the seasonal trades are largely an illusion, and they sink down to something like the general level of yearly earnings in the steady trades. High wages and high earnings are not the same, though sometimes assumed to be such when we think only of demand and supply.

But periodicity is not uncertainty. It comes around regularly. It can be calculated in advance. The amount of unemployment can be discounted. The high wages in the busy season are a rough compensation for idleness in the off season. Uncertainty is different. It cannot be even roughly compensated and is bound up in the unpredictable ebb and flow of prosperity and depression, and in the rise and fall of each individual business undertaking.

The effort to regularize business is not new. The dove-tailing of the coal and ice business, the discounts on orders in the dull seasons, the working to stock in the dull season, all and more of them are old ideas. But it is a new idea and a new impulse that seeks scientifically to regularize business in order to build up goodwill in the labor market.

Prior to this idea the main thought was to keep the plant going at full capacity or to keep a skeleton organization of the higher grades of employees. If 2000 men can be kept together, then 10,000 can be added by advertising when business picks up and can be dropped when it falls off. But if labor turnover is itself expensive, then it might pay to invest some thought and money in keeping the 10,000 together.

The dove-tailing is then more carefully figured out, and the unrecognized gaps are discovered and filled. Workmen are trained for diversified work, so that they can change from one product to a different one. If they earn less at this substitute work, they are even subsidized by a retainer charged up to the cost of the principal or more profitable product. They are paid for versatility as well as for output. The number of short-time jobs is reduced in one direction and enlarged in other directions. The work is arranged to come along in a steady flow instead of bunches. An "emergency squadron" of all-round workers is trained to help out the workers or departments that get behind, instead of leaving it to the foremen to hurry them up. Where the repair gang goes around to fix up machinery when it breaks down, the emergency squadron goes around to fix up goodwill.[1]

If all of these methods fail, then, instead of laying-off some of the workmen, all of them are put on short-time. This is the significance of the "basic eight-hour day." It is not an absolute eight-hour day, and much of the argument against reducing the hours of labor is wasted when the "basic day" rather than the absolute day is proposed.

Almost every industry, including agriculture, might be put on the "basic eight-hour day" at once, requiring only a little more care in time-keeping and supervision. During the first eight hours, regular time is paid and then time-and-a-half for overtime. This is almost the universal practice in trade-union agreements. It permits by pre-arrangement an increased output in the busy season, by adding more hours at higher rates of pay per hour, instead of more men at the same rates, and permits both a reduction in hours and a reduction in labor-cost when business falls off, but without laying off men. If labor turnover is expensive, then the basic eight-hour day is economical and profitable.

The basic eight-hour day also meets, by arrangement in advance, one of the puzzling facts in the psychology of labor. Why is it that workmen are

[1] Consult Slichter, *The Turnover of Factory Labor.*

not willing to take lower rates of pay by the hour or piece in the dull season? If the employer must cut prices and offer discounts in order to induce sales when business falls off, or endeavors to stock up in order to furnish steady employment, why should not labor take its share of the off-season or hard-time burden and do likewise?

It would seem to be simply a question of alternatives. Labor does take its share of the burden of hard times and dull seasons, in one way if not in another. If one-half the force is laid off, they carry the whole of the burden and the other half carries none of it. But if the entire force works half-time the burden is distributed. Workmen seem to prefer the former alternative. The fact that some of them are out of work and others getting high wages seems less obnoxious than for all of them to be at work at lower wages. This was not apparently their attitude before trade unionism began to influence the minds of workers, and is often not their attitude where trade unionism has not yet taken hold. Sometimes it is thought that the workman feels it to be beneath his dignity to work for less in the dull season than the standard scale in the busy season. This is a first impression. Back of it is experience and competition. In order to bring about a return to the higher rate of wages when the good season returns, all competitors must act substantially in unison. The wage-earner who works at the lower scale in the dull season is not in a position to insist on the higher scale in the busy season, and his employer is not likely to pay it unless a sufficient number of workers insist. And those employers who do advance to the higher scale must face the competition of those who do not.

In the clothing trades of New York, during several years, it was this situation that brought on the unorganized strikes at the beginning of each busy season. The new prices would be made in mass meetings for the new season and then, as the dull season approached, competition and unemployment would bring down the piece-prices until a new season and another set of mass meetings restored them. In the busy season all of them were working long hours at high piece-rates, and in the dull season all were working short hours at low piece-rates.[1]

In other seasonal trades the experience is similar, though less dramatic. It is not loss of dignity, but loss of control, that impels the workman to insist, if he can, on the busy price in the dull season. Not unless all competing wage-earners move together in the ups and downs of business can this psychology of bargaining be seriously modified.

But the basic six-hour day or eight-hour day, with time-and-a-half or double-time for overtime, does exactly this thing for workers, when paid by the day. It reduces the hours in dull times, and, by pre-arrangement, reduces the rate of wages per day more than it reduces the hours. Thus it reduces both hours and labor-cost of the product in dull seasons and hard times. This reduction in cost, however, stops at the six-hour or eight-hour level. There is no sufficient reason, if the eight-hour level does not furnish enough elasticity, why the basic seven-hour day or basic six-hour day should not be adopted in those industries where experience shows that employment in off seasons or hard times gets down to thirty-five or forty hours a week.

[1] See Commons, *Trade Unionism and Labor Problems*, pp. 316–335.

Then, when the basic hour day is adopted for day workers, it is but a matter of percentages or differentials added to the piece-rates for piece workers, so that the piece-rates also shall, by pre-arrangement, advance when the hours increase and be reduced when hours are reduced. The basic hour day for day workers and its corresponding differential percentages for piece workers are a modified form of profit sharing, since, in the busy season or prosperous times when there is more work for the employee and more profit for the employer, not only the hours are increased but also the rates of pay per hour and per piece are also increased, and *vice versa.*

Yet too much may be paid for security. Employers may exact too high a price for it. If the price is perpetual low wages, the price is too high. If the price is systematic overtime in order to earn living wages, the price is too high. The basic eight-hour or six-hour day is a good enough theory, when it is used solely for the purpose of providing elasticity. It is vicious if used to reduce earnings and not restore them. It is good enough to tide over depression and to provide for emergencies and to distribute the burden of unemployment. It is abused if it leads to low wages and systematic overtime. It is exactly this possibility of abuse that in the end compels labor unions and legislation to set the absolute maximum hours of labor, which cannot be abused, regardless of emergencies or fluctuations in employment.[1]

[1] Commons and Andrews, *Principles of Labor Legislation,* pp. 204–260. See also *Docket* 37, National War Labor Board, Molders v. Wheeling Mold and Foundry Company (1918); reprinted in *American Federationist,* November, 1918, p. 1000.

The theory of trade unionism meets insecurity by reducing hours or restricting output. Apparently, if there is not enough work to go around, it is pure hoggishness for some to work long hours while others are unemployed, or to take the work from others by speeding up and doing it all yourself. Short hours and reduced output make work for the unemployed.

The theory is good enough in hard times or dull seasons, and indeed is a sound theory when there is not enough work to go around. It serves to *distribute* the limited total amount of work.

But the theory is not good enough to meet the fluctuations of industry as a whole. These fluctuations are changes in the *total amount* of all kinds of products that are produced, and the fluctuations spread over the whole world at about the same time. There would be just about as much unemployment on a universal eight-hour day as on a universal twelve-hour day, and just about as much if everybody worked half as hard as he does, or twice as hard. For unemployment goes by fluctuations. It comes and goes by seasons or by prosperity and depression throughout the world.

If we had a universal eight-hour day in time of prosperity, it would have to be reduced to seven hours or six hours, or less, in time of depression, in order to distribute the reduced total amount of work. Elasticity has to be provided somewhere to meet these fluctuations. The elasticity may be provided by laying off a part of the force in hard times and taking them back in good times, or by reducing hours all around in hard times and increasing them in good times. The one method is the method of unemployment for some, the other the method of distributing unemployment and regularizing employment for all. Not until some method is found to stop the world's fluctuations of prosperity and depression as a whole can industry avoid the necessity of choosing one or the other of these unfortunate alternatives.

The theory of socialism offers this method, and the weightiest argument for socialism is the unemployment produced by capitalism. The socialistic theory, indeed, may be said to sacrifice everything else in order to get security of employment. And, to the unemployed or half employed workers, why should they not sacrifice everything else? What is the use of private initiative without bread and butter? What is the use of liberty and efficiency without security? Why should employers be permitted to use unemployment as a club to drive down wages and to control even the opinions and politics of workingmen?

Surely, security of employment, or at least security of minimum earnings in time of depression, is one of the tests of the stability of capitalism. Fluctuations in industry and employment are a condition that must be met in one way or another. Unhappily, these world fluctuations make it impossible to look forward to a fixed regular income or regular work. Overwork and big earnings in busy seasons and good times, underwork and small earnings in dull seasons and hard times, are the most serious defect of industry, and the one hardest to meet. But while they make impossible a fixed regular income, they do not make impossible a much greater security when once attention is seriously directed toward it.

The matter is one for investigation and ingenuity

in each particular case.   Scientific management accomplished unbelievable results when once engineers and business men began to experiment according to its principles.   Scientific goodwill may likewise be ingenious when managers and employers begin to experiment with it.   The foremost of its principles is security—the privilege of looking forward to a secure income—and security not for a few but for all.   The employer, or association of employers, or nation of employers, that sets its engineers, accountants, statisticians, scientific managers, along with the labor organizations and shop committees, to work out the problem of security of employment, or at least security of earnings, is rescuing capitalism at the point where it stands most in need of goodwill.

IX

LABOR MARKET

Goodwill is a competitive advantage. Its value consists in ability to get or keep desirable customers or workers away from rivals. The best workers, on the average, are not the unemployed but those already holding good jobs. The labor turnover does not show itself strongly among this class of workers. It occurs among the newly hired, the less skilled, the boys, young men, girls, and those holding the less desirable jobs.

It is here that the public interest also concentrates. Those who have steady desirable jobs are, of course, not moving about, except occasionally when they can evidently better their position. Theirs is indeed a normal and desirable turnover, for it is a necessary alternative to promotion. But, for the others, their excessive turnover is a detriment to themselves, their employers and the nation.

The natural and most satisfactory method of recruiting new workmen is through their friends or acquaintances already employed in the establishment. This method works a treble benefit. It is a compliment to the worker if he is asked to recommend somebody; it is a help to the employer in getting a good selection of recruits; and it is a help to the new man or boy in getting over the early period when he is

74

most likely to be discouraged. It attaches both the old and the new worker to the firm.

But this method assumes that the establishment is already a good place to work, and it gets good results because good men are already employed whose recommendations can be relied upon. In short, it is simply the natural method by which goodwill is always built up. An establishment is fortunate, and indeed has about reached the perfection of goodwill, if all of its recruiting for new help is accomplished in this way. It has a steady, loyal force and it grows by getting new men who are steady and loyal.

No business firm is quite so fortunate as this, and not many desire to recruit their entire force in this way. It applies to skilled or semi-skilled men and to boys beginning as learners, and not generally to common laborers. Even for these better positions it cannot take care of emergencies. And even at its best it runs the risk of cliques and clans in the shop.

By far the largest source of supply in general is that of applicants seeking work, either at the gates or at employment offices. This means a constant over-supply of labor relative to demand, a "reserve army" of labor unemployed but ready to be employed.

Even in the most prosperous times when there seems to be a real scarcity of labor, this reserve army is not taken up entirely but shrinks only to an "irreducible minimum."[1] The lowest number of unemployed among the trade unions of New York over a period of twelve years was in October, 1906, when it was 5.6 per cent of the total number of all who reported.

[1] Beveridge, W. H., *Unemployment* (1910), p. 69.

The highest number of unemployed was 40 per cent in January, 1915.[1] These are mostly skilled laborers. For the unskilled and semi-skilled, if records were kept, the irreducible minimum would probably appear much above 6 per cent.

Here, again, it was the necessities of war that forced public attention and public organization to take care of this reserve army of labor. At the very height of the "drive" for more labor, a report made to the American Federation of Labor in November, 1917, showed large numbers of unemployed in different parts of the country.[2] Men were scarce in some sections, out of work in others.

Ohio was the first state to seize this problem correctly.[3] Other states set out to obtain a doubtful census of workers, but Ohio set out to organize the labor market. Within the space of two weeks, 21 free state employment offices were established, each one located with special reference to railway centers. A central clearing house was set up at Columbus. The long distance telephone bills reached $20.00 to $30.00 a day. The state superintendent is at the telephone continuously, communicating with the 20 branch offices. When twenty thousand men were wanted to build the cantonment at Chilicothe, the contractors were warned not to advertise for help. Advertising would flood the market at Chilicothe and

[1] New York Department of Labor, *Special Bulletin*, No. 85, July, 1917, pp. 25, 50.

[2] *Report of Proceedings of American Federation of Labor*, 1917, p. 440.

[3] See articles by W. M. Leiserson, *Monthly Review*, U. S. Bureau of Labor Statistics, April, 1918, pp. 53–63; *The Survey*, April 20, 1918, p. 65.

rob it at spots elsewhere.   It would bring thousands of men before the work was ready and let them wait in idleness.   Neither was the contractor to engage with private employment offices.   He agreed to hire all his help through the Columbus office and to call for help only when needed and in the exact number needed. Every call was in effect a contract.   The Columbus office then required each of the branch offices to register all available labor and to get local employers to furnish lists of skilled help whom they might temporarily release.   Then, for a day when the contractor wanted two thousand men, exactly two thousand men were pro-rated over the entire state by telephone; each local office was ordered to send its quota; no section of the state was robbed of labor; no workman made a trip before his work was ready for him, and the contractor received exactly the number he was ready to put to work.   Likewise, on another day when one hundred were wanted, or five hundred, and so on.

The same was true when the cantonment was finished.   The workmen all were registered.   Work was found for them in the state or other states and they left their Chilicothe jobs to go directly to other jobs waiting for them.

So simple and common-sense a plan of organization ought to appeal to employers but it did not until the crisis of a war overrode their prejudices or broke their inertia, and even then, it was only in the single state of Ohio that the state authorities were daring enough to seize the opportunity to enlist the right executive ability and to spend the necessary amount of money.

For employers are accustomed to advertise when they want help, not realizing that advertising either pulls workmen away from other employers or assumes the existence of a reserve army unemployed. From the individual standpoint, advertising for labor may be successful; from the public standpoint it may be wasteful.

Or employers are accustomed to rely on private enterprise, which in this case is the competing private employment offices, not realizing that these have no interest in conserving labor but merely in getting as many fees as possible from as many laborers as possible.

Or, finally, employers' associations have their own employment bureaus created to help them in fighting trade unions, and if the public is allowed to set up free public offices and supplant their association bureaus, then their power as an organized class over labor as a class is threatened.

For these various reasons of inertia, prejudice, or loss of power, employers have either not taken hold or have actually obstructed the only possible method by which the labor market as a whole can be organized in the public interest as against private interest or class interest.

Somewhat different have been the obstacles set up by labor, organized and unorganized. Public employment offices in various states and cities have been considered by labor to be the special perquisite of labor, created to help labor find employment. Hence, labor must control the offices. This means that labor politicians who can get the labor vote are placed in charge of the offices. Naturally employers do not patronize them, and they degenerate into a "hang out" for casual, inferior, and even pauper labor.

Even when the crisis of war was upon the nation and the disorganized labor market threatened military collapse, it required over a year for the trade unionist Secretary of Labor to be willing to set aside the labor politicians and the trade unionist pensioners who had attempted to install a federal system of employment offices. Finally, the Secretary authorized the Ohio system to be adopted and extended throughout the nation.

The things essential in a public employment system are competent officials and organization of capital and labor. The two go together. Expert officials cannot be obtained unless the position offers security and promotion. This means a national system, the training of young men and women as beginners, the transfer, promotion and salary increase in higher positions through to the very top of the system.

To get such officials they cannot be appointed by trade unionists, nor by employers, nor even by a civil service commission. The latter gives necessary aid by its written examinations, in eliminating the evidently unfit, or fills successfully the merely clerical positions, but the selection and appointment of those who have the responsibility of bringing employer and employee together and filling the jobs by workers who fit the jobs, can be made only under the joint supervision and consent of organized employers and organized workers. The responsibility of these employment officials is great. Not only must they be "fair" to both sides in the conflict of capital and labor, but there must be not even a suspicion of unfairness. They are in a position evidently to give a preference to trade unionists or to strike breakers, and as soon as they do either, or are suspected of leaning toward either, their usefulness is gone. Civil service examinations alone cannot bring out this quality of fairness, although they are essential in preparing the way for it. It is a matter of judgment and opinion of those whose conflicting interests are at stake.

This means representative democracy in the civil service. In one way or another organized capital and organized labor must jointly have the final determining voice in the selection and promotion of public employment officers and in the supervision of their work.

When once the organized but opposing interests are then brought together as advisers and supervisors coöperating with the government, they themselves rise above their class conflicts and suspicions. I have seen the employer's representatives under these circumstances even join in the selection of a trade unionist and a "card" socialist for these important positions, and have seen the union representatives join in selecting a non-union contractor or employer.

For "class conflict" is not irrepressible. It can be bridged over at strategic points. But it cannot be hurried or rushed. It means consent, and consent takes time.

The instincts of bureaucracy often stand in the way of this deliberative partnership. State or government officials and civil service commissions instinctively feel that they know their own business and are impatient in submitting their judgment to unofficial civilians. They select and promote subordinates according to their own ideas. In this way bureaucracy grows. But in this delicate matter of class conflict, at the strategic points where it is liable to break out, bureaucracy breaks down. It requires to be supplemented by organized democracy.

In running a public employment office the government is "going out after business." Its patrons are employers and laborers. If it cannot hold their patronage it does not get the business. Employers cease to patronize and workers look elsewhere for jobs. In the stress of war, when the government is almost the sole employer, the government officials can insist that the public offices alone shall be patronized. In times of peace, it is only the day-to-day confidence of private employers that they can get the kind of help they want, that keeps the office on its feet. If employers run their own private agencies they, of course, are not disturbed by lack of confidence, for their control is complete. If they patronize the public offices they abandon insofar a powerful weapon devised to combat trade unionism. Both trade unionism and bureaucracy may well admit employers to partnership on equal terms in controlling the offices, for only in this way can there be permanently maintained the first great essential in regularizing employment in the interest of both labor and the nation, a national employment system enjoying a monopoly as complete as that of the post office. And employers and employers' associations should lend their aid in building up this type of public employment offices, for of all the agencies that demoralize labor and intensify the illwill of labor to-

6

ward capital, none is more unscrupulously effective than the competing private employment offices that live on the fees of unemployed workers.[1]

[1] For further details and discussion, see Commons and Andrews, *Principles of Labor Legislation*, pp. 261–293; *American Labor Legislation Review*, November, 1915, March, 1918; *Final Report of Commission on Industrial Relations*, p. 170 *ff*; *Employment Service Bulletin*, United States Department of Labor, Monthly, beginning January 29, 1918.

X

INSURANCE

Unions affiliated with the American Federation of Labor reported that they had paid, in 1917, about $3,000,000 in death benefits and only $2,400,000 on account of strikes. Only seven unions did not report death benefits.[1]

These benefits are small in amount. Their average is something over $100.00.[2] Provision for the family after the death of the worker is seldom possible out of these meagre amounts. Only 23 unions reported sick benefits, amounting to $840,000. Measured by the amount of money expended, more important to organized workers than provision for strikes or sickness is the craving to be decently buried.

So it is with workers in general. Thirty-eight million policies are outstanding of the kind known as "industrial insurance."[3] Probably thirty million workers hold these policies. They are a form of life insurance. The average amount of the policies is about $130.00. They, too, are provision for decent burial.

The expense of conducting industrial insurance is enormous. In 1916, a leading company received

[1] *Report of Proceedings of American Federation of Labor*, 1917, pp. 33, 36.

[2] *Twenty-third Annual Report of the Commissioner of Labor* (1908), pp. 213–219.

[3] *Insurance Year Book*, 1918.

about $62,000,000 in premiums and returned $29,-000,000 to policy-holders.[1] For every dollar paid for insurance about 53 cents was needed to meet expenses and profits.

This must be so, for industrial insurance is the smallest of retail insurance. Premiums are paid weekly, or when the pay envelope is full. The weekly premiums are 10, 15, 25 cents, and the insurance agent collects them in cash from house to house.

The lapses, too, are many. Unemployment, sickness, accident, stops the payment of premiums. The number of lapses in ten years has been estimated at nearly two-thirds of the number of policies written.[2]

Besides the funeral benefits of organized labor and the funeral benefits of industrial insurance, there are also the unknown millions of assessment policies of the unknown hundreds or thousands of sickness and death fraternal societies.[3]

The heavy expense of retail insurance suggests the adoption of wholesale insurance. The employer of labor is naturally in a position to buy insurance wholesale for his employees. The first policy of this kind was taken out in 1912 by a mail-order house.[4] Whether this class of insurance is written with a commercial insurance company, or whether the great

[1] See *Financial Report for the Year Ending December* 31, 1917, Prudential Insurance Company, as made to the Wisconsin Insurance Commission.

[2] Rubinow, *Social Insurance*, p. 421.

[3] See Sydenstricker, E., "Existing Agencies for Health Insurance in the United States," *Proceedings of the Conference on Social Insurance.* Bulletin of the Bureau of Labor Statistics, No. 212, p. 430.

[4] Morris, E. B., *Group Life Insurance and Its Possible Development.* Address before the Casualty Actuarial and Statistical Society, 1917.

employing corporation finds that it can more economically "carry its own insurance" is immaterial. If the employer carries the insurance himself, it is known as an "establishment fund," or "self-insurance," and is a part of what has come to be known as a "welfare system." If an insurance company carries the insurance it is known as "group insurance." The characteristic of group insurance, as now written, is that it picks out certain definite actuarial items from the larger welfare system and deals with them as a separate problem. These are life insurance, old age pensions, perhaps also premature disability, and sometimes sickness insurance.

The recent rapid spread of group insurance, whether establishment funds or commercial insurance, shows that it fits a gap in industry newly recognized and keenly felt. The financial inducement to the employer is the reduction of his labor turnover. As stated by one of the insurance companies in its advertising circulars, group insurance brings "a closer and more intimate relation between employer and employee, the existence of contentment and happiness in the employee and his family; the cessation of strife and misunderstanding; the production of incentive and initiative; the amelioration of the living conditions of the widow and the orphan; the betterment of community social conditions; the encouragement and valuation of the energies in men that count and the actual return, measure for measure, in dividends."[1]

Indeed, if these objects can be brought about by setting aside a premium of 1 to 2 per cent on the pay-roll, then the investment is likely to be more

[1] *The Employer and The Employee*, pamphlet.

profitable than any other expenditure of a similar sum.

For, group insurance is both elastic and cheap. It can be written to fit any of the circumstances or wishes of any employer. Usually, it is outside the accident compensation law. It may cover only life insurance. If so, it usually covers one year's wages of each employee, payable in monthly installments. The worker's earnings thus are made to continue uninterrupted for a year after his death, for the benefit of his family. The employer may insure every employee, from the president of the corporation to the casual laborer. The protection may be graded according to length of service. It may be restricted to those who have been with the company a year, or six months, or one month, or may take effect for each worker on the day he goes to work.

The policy may carry other features in addition to life insurance. It may carry an old age pension, beginning at sixty-five or other age, running for the remainder of life, and fixed at any amount determined by the employer. It may provide for invalidity, or permanent disability, that is, for premature old age arising from any cause not otherwise safeguarded. It may, indeed, include sickness or temporary disability, though the policies written with insurance companies have seldom gone this far.

The elasticity of group insurance is further evident in that it may be made, and usually is made, universal for all employees in the establishment, without medical examination or selection of risks. It takes the industry and the workers as it finds them, and excludes no one on account of physical defects not otherwise sufficient to exclude him from employment. And the cost of this life insurance is figured at about 1 to 1½ per cent on the pay-roll. The premium payments are made monthly, rising and falling with the pay-roll.

Presumably, the workers are insured only while actually working, and if laid off through lack of work, or if absent through sickness or other cause, the insurance lapses, but begins again when work begins. These are matters of detail, adjustable as may be desired within the limits of the rate of premium which the employer decides to appropriate and the extent of the inducement which he decides to offer to his employees in consideration of continuing in his service.

For the object of group insurance is the goodwill of labor. Generally, wherever adopted, whether by means of an insurance policy or by means of self-insurance and establishment funds, it is believed to be followed by a reduction in labor turnover, or by what is equally valuable, a reduction in strikes and in the power of organized labor to attract employees away from their allegiance.

This is, indeed, the ultimate test. Does group insurance promote the laborer's welfare at the cost of his liberty? Liberty is not an empty idea, but is the laborer's means of getting higher wages when times are good and employers are competing for labor. The laborer's liberty may be worthless to him in hard times but it is valuable in good times. The well-known increase of labor turnover in good times is a rise in the market value of liberty.

Undoubtedly, and perhaps without exception, employers maintain that their group insurance and welfare systems are an addition over and above wages. They instruct their foremen and employment managers to pay the market rate of wages, and not to use welfare or death benefits or group insurance as a talking point to get below the market rate. But the real question is, what is its effect on the market rate itself?

Goodwill is a competitive advantage. If it does not hold the worker's allegiance against the drawing power of competing employers, then it yields no advantage. Life insurance, old age pensions, even invalidity insurance, may not be strong enough to hold the young man. The benefit to him is remote and dim, but the wages offered elsewhere are nearby and vivid. As he grows older and acquires a family the expected benefits come nearer and brighter, and the wages offered elsewhere are comparatively less attractive.

If all competing employers provided exactly the same benefits, and if the insurance took effect on the very day when the worker goes to work, then the thing that would draw the older worker, as well as the younger, away from one employer to another would be the higher present wages and not the higher future benefits. The employer would have to raise his wages in order to keep his workers. But as long as only a few employers carry group insurance and others do not, then the few need not raise their wages to the same extent as others, in order to hold their workers.

One or 2 per cent increase in wages is a very small increase in good times when wages are going up

5 per cent or 10 per cent or even more. If a group insurance employer is able by his promise of future benefits to hold his employees without advancing their wages as rapidly as others do, then it is his employees who are paying his insurance premiums. It only needs that their wages lag 1 or 2 per cent behind the advancing wages of other employees on the labor market in order to shift the cost of the insurance upon them.

That this is the effect of old age, life insurance and invalidity systems of welfare is well known to trade union organizers. They find it difficult to organize the workers who expect these benefits by remaining where they are. Their promises that the union will get them even much higher wages *now*, perhaps at the cost of a strike as a last resort, has usually very little drawing power against the prospect of forfeiting the *future* benefits by quitting their jobs. For this reason, mainly, trade unions are hostile to employers' group insurance and welfare systems.

Their hostility is probably misplaced. Group insurance and welfare systems are coming, because, like accident compensation, they fill the next largest gap in the struggle of capital and labor. It is only a little less bitter and humiliating that employers as a class should use up their workers for profit and then neglect them and their families in old age, disability, and death, than it is that they should grind profits out of accidents. Public opinion, public welfare, sympathy, must surely support every employer as well as the ingenuity and enterprise of the casualty companies, when they make this next notable advance toward goodwill between employer and employee.

The drawback is that they cannot make it universal. The backward, indifferent, incompetent or small employer should be brought up to the level of these pioneers. Only compulsory insurance can bring this about. If all employers are required by law to insure all their workers against death, old age and premature old age, then not only is this form of welfare made universal but it cannot be practised at the cost of liberty. The workers then are freed from that menace which now threatens to play upon their anxiety for decent burial and for the future of family and self in order to tie them to their jobs.

In the interests of the freedom of labor the hostility of labor organizers should be directed, not against group insurance in itself, but against insurance which is not universal. Eventually, as voluntary group insurance enlarges and its effects in restricting liberty are more clearly recognized, it may be expected that trade unions will more generally approve compulsory insurance made universal by law.

Compulsory insurance, like compulsory accident compensation, enlarges liberty by restraining it in other directions. And employers as a class get more liberty in the right direction than they lose in the wrong direction, for then the cut-throat competition of those who are indifferent or incompetent is eliminated at the point where they intensify class antagonism and prevent others from rising above their level.

Sometimes the objection is raised that compulsory insurance of this kind implies that the government must go into the insurance business and greatly increase the force of government employees. This is a mistake. Compulsory group insurance merely requires all employers to do what others are now doing without compulsion. They may still insure with the private casualty companies, or may organize employer's mutuals, or the largest may carry their own insurance and establishment funds if financially responsible. It is a different proposition for the state to go into the insurance business and administer a fund like a private company. States may experiment in this business. There is much to be said in favor of a state fund, when efficiently conducted, instead of commercial insurance.[1] But that is a different question. The essential thing that the state needs to do is to determine by law the minimum amount of benefits to be paid to the workers or their families and then require employers to take out insurance if they are not financially responsible. As is done in accident compensation, the state would set up arbitration boards to hear and decide the disputes that might come up.

[1] See arguments before New York Legislature, April 2, 1918, by F. Spencer Baldwin, Manager of the New York State Insurance Fund, and Thomas J. Duffy, Chairman Ohio State Industrial Commission. New York State Federation of Labor, 1918.

XI

HEALTH

The physical examination of the first two and one-half million young men for the army revealed about 30 per cent who were physically unfit. The percentages varied widely for different states, the lowest percentage being 14, the highest 47.[1] This was the first great American survey of health. The defects and incipient diseases there revealed were either unknown to the young men themselves or neglected.

It is roughly estimated that, on the average, working people in the United States lose eight or nine days a year on account of sickness.[2] They and their employers probably lose as much more on account of slow work, poor work, accidents, and premature old age caused by keeping at work while they are half-sick. The money loss is incalculable but must be enormous.[3]

A certain corporation with four thousand employees,

[1] *Report of the Provost Marshal General to the Secretary of War, On the First Draft under the Selective-Service Act,* 1917 (1918), p. 83.

[2] B. S. Warren and Edgar Sydenstricker, *Public Health Bulletin No. 76,* p. 6. Cf. Metropolitan Life Insurance Company, *Community Sickness Surveys; Proceedings of the Conference on Social Insurance,* Bulletin of the United States Bureau of Labor Statistics, No. 212 (1917), p. 643.

[3] Computations have been made by Fisher, *Report on National Vitality* (1909). *Bulletin* 30 of the Committee of One Hundred on National Health, pp. 119–120; Rubinow, *Social Insurance* (1913), pp. 214, 222.

some seven years ago, started a compulsory sick benefit society for its employees. Every employee is required to pay 50 cents a month into the fund, and the corporation adds an equal amount. No employee is taken on without a physical examination. The company stands to lose a considerable amount of money expended in training employees, and each man is an investment. On this account the risks in the benefit society are selected risks, and the dollar a month for each employee goes further than it would for unselected risks. It has been found that, while on the average the estimated time lost through sickness by workpeople is eight or nine days a year, this company has reduced the lost time to four and one-half days. Since the average earnings of the men are about $3.00 a day, it needs only a saving of two or three days in lost time to enable the workmen to make up the dues of $6.00 a year in the benefit society.

But the benefit society takes care, also, of most of the ailments of the worker's family, and when, at the end of seven years, it was found that a reserve fund of $60,000 had accumulated, the society, without additional dues, added the care of the mother at child-birth and all obstetrical treatment. So that at a cost of $12.00 a year for each employee, all of his own medical care and that of his family are provided.

It was found at first that the workers did not sufficiently call upon the physicians of the society in the early stages of illness, and so the society stationed physicians at each shop every morning where the workmen could consult them without extra time or fear of being considered a nuisance. In short, the society encouraged the very thing that is often raised as an objection to universal health insurance, namely, the multiplication of unnecessary calls upon the doctor.

And this is, indeed, the prime object of health insurance—not the cure of illness after it has set in, but the prevention of illness. And the only complete preventor of illness is the doctor. The government of the United States furnishes President Wilson with a high-grade physician who attends him constantly, not with medicines but with advice. A millionaire has his private physician. This benefit society does for four thousand workers daily what the nation or great wealth does for the President or the millionaire.

The benefit society engages its physicians and surgeons on part-time contracts, the minimum compensation being at a salary rate of $3000 a year. The physicians have also their private practice. The society has constantly in its service two nurses for home visiting, but does not pay for hospital care.

The primary object of this association is sickness prevention. But when sickness cannot be prevented, the loss of wages is partly made up by cash benefits.

Here is the difficult problem of health insurance. At one extreme, if a cash benefit is paid equal or approximate to the lost wages, the premium on feigned sickness is so great as to amount to a general demoralization of the entire labor force. At the other extreme, if no sick benefit is paid, the anxiety of the worker over the loss of wages is a serious impediment to recovery and to that state of mind which is willing to lay off long enough to get well.

This benefit society has hit upon a workable medium

between these two extremes. No cash benefit is
paid during the first seven days laid off. Then $1.00
a day is paid for 100 days. Then 50 cents a day for
the second 100 days. Then, if permanent invalidity
ensues, the lump sum of $150.00 provided in the by-
laws, is paid to the worker, and thereafter he both
loses his employment with the company and his
membership in the society. A funeral benefit also
is paid.

· The society is strictly a temporary sickness society
and does not provide for life insurance, for superannuation, or for permanent disability. As a strictly
sickness society it recompenses the worker for his
lost wages to the extent of perhaps one-third or one-
fourth of his loss, and thus relieves his anxiety in
part but not enough to tempt malingering.[1]

What does the corporation gain by means of this
society? It spends some $25,000 a year at the rate
of $6.00 for each employee, or say one-half of 1
per cent. on its pay-roll, and what does it get in return
that justifies the management in their reports to
the stockholders?

How shall we measure the intangible asset, goodwill? How shall we measure the money value of
good health?

In the first place we must measure it partly by

---

[1] The most complete and detailed analysis of the features of an Employees' Benefit Association is the series of articles by W. L. Chandler
in *Industrial Management*, beginning February, 1918. A voluntary
association has, perhaps, an advantage over the compulsory system
above described. It is not intended to close employment against
those incapable of passing a physical examination. See By-Laws,
Employee's Mutual Benefit Association, Milwaukee Electric Railway
and Light Company.

faith. It rests in part on the "will to believe." No measurement can be devised that will satisfy the short-sighted or greedy stockholder. Goodwill and good health are an overhead. They belong to *l'esprit de corps*, the spirit of the going concern, the morale of confidence and hope.

And a benefit society cannot be separated out and measured apart from the other intangible factors that go to make up goodwill. th Ife employees are convinced or even suspicious that the benefit society is imposed in order to tie them to their jobs and to shift over to them in low wages the money contributed by the company under the name of benefits, then, instead of an asset it becomes a liability. I have known of benefit societies which caused strikes instead of goodwill. The very same schedule of dues, physical examinations, medical care and cash benefits, in the hands of one management will win loyalty, in the hands of a different management—illwill. There is no invariable standard of measurement that can pick out the benefit society and measure it independently of the other parts of the company's policy toward labor.

We may pick out symptoms and they are good as far as they go, but not conclusive. We may show the reduction in lost time from improved health, the reduction in accidents from improved attention, the reduction in turnover from improved loyalty, the increase in output from improved vigor, but these are partial and not convincing. Each establishment must be judged as a whole and by itself. All of the facts and all of the parts must be put together, and then a large element of faith in humanity, of enthusiasm for human welfare, of pride in good work, and even of patriotism in contributing to the physical and moral health of the nation, must be added before health insurance of one's employees will appeal to the management or the stockholders as a good investment.

Here is exactly where compulsory health insurance comes in.[1] Only a small proportion of all employers and corporations are sufficiently educated, interested, public spirited, and financially able to adopt health insurance for their employees. The state can never hope to bring the others up to the level of the most progressive, but it can establish minimum standards and require all to come up to a certain lower level. If this is wisely done, then the more progressive are in a position to go as far ahead of the legal minimum as their ingenuity and enterprise may suggest.

There have been many and various proposals put forward for universal health insurance.[2] It can hardly be expected that all the details can be worked out satisfactorily in advance. There is room for many experiments and much ingenuity. Especially must any satisfactory plan be based on existing American conditions and afford room for private initiative in working out the details.

[1] Arguments pro and con of health insurance will be found in Commons and Andrews, *Principles of Labor Legislation*, p. 385 ff. See references there cited: Hoffman, *Facts and Fallacies of Compulsory Health Insurance*, published by Prudential Press, Newark, N. J.; Rubinow, *Social Insurance* (1913); American Association for Labor Legislation publications.

[2] See especially draft of bill introduced by Senator Nicoll, New York Senate, February 18, 1918. Also model bill recommended by a committee of the American Association for Labor Legislation, 131 E. 23d St., New York.

7

Most of the American states are already in a position to authorize and require these experiments to be made. They have their accident compensation commissions, their schedules of indemnity, their organization of compulsory accident insurance. To these may be added health insurance by requiring of all employers a minimum provision for medical and hospital supplies and treatment and a minimum attendance of qualified physicians and nurses.

Whether employees should be required to contribute equally with the employer depends on the extent to which the benefits are carried. If the families of wage-earners are included, as well as the wage-earner himself, the employee should evidently contribute. If the employer is already carrying group insurance or a fund for old age, disability and death, the employee should evidently contribute to the sickness fund. The essential thing is that, where employees contribute they have equal representation in the management.

If their plan meets the minimum standards of the law and shows the financial security required for an insurance scheme, it is then certified by the state authorities and the association is permitted to proceed. The state authority retains supervision and acts as an appellate court in the settlement of disputes.

These are perhaps the essential minimum legal requirements. Over and above them remains opportunity for all or any voluntary schemes, designed by employers, trade unions or fraternal societies. Fraternal societies and trade unions find their field in the provision for cash benefits. It would probably be preferable that the cash benefits should be left entirely to voluntary schemes, and that the legal minimum standards should make no requirement whatever of cash benefits in case of temporary disability through illness.

Two practical considerations lead to this suggestion: if cash benefits are required by law, then the thought and energies of employers, employees and state officials are diverted away from the prime object of health insurance, which is sickness prevention with its medical and hospital care and early diagnosis. If cash benefits are required by law, then innumerable disputes arise as to the amount of benefits; the dangerous menace of malingering is forced into the problem; suspicion and invidious investigations of individuals are fomented by law. But with cash benefits eliminated from the requirements of the law, all of the funds and all of the energies of all parties, so far as legislation is concerned, are directed to the single purpose of adequate care for sickness, adequate hospital and medical equipment, and adequate measures of prevention.

Equally important is the other practical consideration. Relieved of medical and hospital care and sickness prevention the voluntary associations of trade unions, fraternal societies, and employers' mutuals have a free and exclusive field for that which they can do much better, the provision for cash benefits.

This field they have begun to cultivate. Almost none of the local trade unions that provide sick benefits, make any provision for medical and hospital service, or for regular employment of physicians, or for the prevention and early diagnosis of disease. If they employ a physician it is to prevent malingering.[1] Their sick benefits are nearly always simply cash benefits. They leave the field of protection and prevention, medical and hospital treatment, practically untouched, and limit themselves to the field of cash payments at time of sickness. A compulsory system of cash benefits would interfere with their work. A compulsory system of insurance for medical and hospital care not only would not interfere with the work of unions, fraternals and mutuals, but would strengthen the appeal for voluntary cash insurance.

On the other hand, health insurance, covering the first three months or six months of sickness, should be combined with group insurance or establishment funds for old age, death and permanent disability beginning at the end of the health insurance period. Here cash benefits are evidently required, and are not likely to be provided by other existing agencies. And, most of all, here the menace of malingering no longer holds as a valid objection. The principles of group insurance have already been worked out scientifically by private insurance companies. Permanent disability begins at the end of say three months or six months illness. Superannuation begins at say sixty or sixty-five or seventy years of age. The amount of the benefits is, of course, determined by the amount of the premiums that seem expedient to be required.

There is a sentimental objection to these plans of

[1] Sydenstricker, E., "Existing Agencies for Health Insurance in the United States," *Proceedings of the Conference on Social Insurance,* Bulletin of the United States Bureau of Labor Statistics, No. 212 (1917), pp. 467, 473.

mandatory insurance. It is said, "Why should an honest, hard working, thrifty, employee be compelled to contribute to a fund to support the thriftless and vicious employee whose illness and disability are brought on by his own fault?" "Why should a prosperous employer be compelled to contribute to the funds that help out the less prosperous, or be compelled to contribute to workmen and their families for whose illness he is not responsible?"

These questions are naturally suggested by the extremely individualistic American way of looking at things. But modern competitive industry, national peril, and solidarity of interest are answering them.

A serious menace to the wages of workingmen is the cut-throat competition of the less competent. If 10 per cent of the workingmen are thriftless and vicious, then the competition of that 10 per cent is a load on the neck of the 90 per cent. They and their unfortunate families are thrown upon the labor market, and it is one of the benefits of universal insurance that it helps in some degree to take them off the market. The honest, thrifty worker is already paying a part of the cost of the thriftless and vicious, but he is paying it through the invisible pressure of competitive wages. Health insurance, properly worked out, is a visible payment designed to remove that invisible pressure.

And why should the employer pay when he is not responsible? This was the very question raised against universal accident compensation. Since that question has been answered, individual employers have been paying for accidents caused by other employers or by their own employees. So it is with health and disability and old age. Employers as a class are concerned with the health and efficiency of labor as a class. They are already paying invisibly for illness and inefficiency. Their costs are already shifted more or less upon the public. To pay openly into insurance funds is but to pay visibly toward removing an indefinite, but actual, invisible expense.

Thus the answer to the individualistic question is the solidarity of interests. Competition distributes, by its unseen but powerful pressure, the accidents, illness and disabilities of labor among all employers, all employees, and the public. Neither the total expense nor the share borne by either can be measured. But health insurance, with disability and superannuation, measures off and distributes among them all a minimum expense for reducing an immeasurable but enormous expense.

But this argument of solidarity, like the argument of individualism, cannot be carried too far. It is as false as the other if pushed to extremes. Carried to the extreme it is socialism, just as individualism carried to its extreme is anarchism. The reasonable man and the reasonable nation must find by experience and wisdom the point where the two principles can be combined and get the maximum value from the combination.

It is for this reason that the principle of solidarity, or compulsory insurance, should go to the extent of only the minimum necessary to get the one essential thing—national health. If properly worked out, this insurance principle enlists in the cause of sickness prevention and national efficiency the most tangible and effective of earthly inducements—the financial inducement. By reducing the amount of sickness and by postponing the period of disability, the monthly insurance premiums are reduced, and can be seen and measured by every employer and every worker.

And it cannot be said that modern employers as a class are not responsible in part for the early disabilities and short working life of laborers as a class. While salaried men, professional men, employers themselves, and those who make an early escape from manual labor, begin to reach their high levels of efficiency at forty years of age, the modern factory worker has passed his zenith at forty. His long hours of work, his compulsory work when ill, his periods of unemployment, his fatigue and confinement are among the outstanding causes. No individual employer is responsible. No individual can do much better than his competitors. All are responsible together, for competition forces them into a solidarity of responsibility. All must therefore work together to meet their joint responsibility. And compulsory insurance, up to a certain point, is the modern method of enforcing joint responsibility.

Perhaps, at no other point will the enforcement of this joint responsibility of employers be more awakening than in the attention it will focus on the evils of the piece-work system. The piece-work, bonus or premium system, enables employers to evade their responsibility for the health and long life of workers. It throws the responsibility on the worker himself for exerting himself. By its continuous nervous strain day after day and year after year, it eventually wears out the worker. It wears out women faster than men, the ambitious faster than the sluggish, and eventually weakens the tissues and admits the germs of disease.

Doubtless "payment by results" is a necessary method of payment, but carried to the extreme of the piece-work system, it is destructive of results through premature disability. At no point in the industrial system is there greater need of focusing the ingenuity and enterprise of employers, of employment managers, engineers and industrial service workers, than at the point of taking a long-life view of piece-work. The system doubtless gets immediate results hour by hour, but somebody must pay for its later results. The employer shifts these later results on the worker himself and on the nation through sickness, premature old age and short life. Mandatory insurance for health, for disability, superannuation and death, not merely requires employers as a class to carry a part of these burdens, but, most of all, induces them as a class to engage their business ability and ingenuity in the direction of reducing the amount of the burden itself by earnestly investigating and then effectively removing the causes that produce the burden.

And this responsibility is not responsibility merely to labor—it is responsibility to the nation. The nation took millions of workers from the factories and shops. The first thing it did was to attend to their health. It gave them an unexpected vigor that factory and shop had suppressed. And when, with these powerful new bodies and this aroused patriotism they fought in Europe for national liberty, they also fought for the nation's business. Shall they afterward go back into the factory and shop and again be subjected

to the competitive deterioration of health? Neither
their own aroused intelligence nor the nation's future
industrial progress will permit it. They have learned
the power of joint action and the spirit of comrade-
ship. The awakened employer, who sees the future,
will surely provide for the future and will arouse his
sluggish fellow-employer. And can he do it in any
other way so effectively as by placing on all employers
the legal duty, first of all, of joining in mutual associations of employer and employee to safeguard the
health and prolong the working life of them all?

XII

THE SHOP

The five or six thousand employees of a manufacturing company went out on strike without previous organization. After several weeks the company made a settlement and took the workers back as a union. The main demand of the strikers was higher wages. This was granted. But the company discovered that what they wanted was control of discipline. The company thought that it had been running its own business, but it discovered that the labor end of its business had been run by foremen and superintendents. The issue with the union turned out to be whether the union or these minor executives should control the discipline.

Wages were the apparent demand. The real grievance was the accumulation of petty complaints, often unfounded, against the minor executives of the company. The company thought that, by granting the demand for wages they could have peace for a while. They found that nearly every rule or command given by their minor executives brought on the menace of a strike. The issue was not wages but discipline. And this is always the issue of unionism.

Soon after the agreement became effective the company relieved the executives of their final power of discipline and established a labor department with a chief who reports direct to the company. The labor department investigates all complaints; recommends to the company a course of action; conducts all negotiations with the union; superintends all hiring and firing; manages the hospital, rest room and welfare work; is responsible for the observance of state and municipal labor laws; endeavors to educate the foremen and workers in conciliation; has direction of all adjustments of wages, piece prices and operating efficiency. In short, discipline is separated from production.

Considerable ingenuity, experimentation and a code of procedure were necessary to make this separation. The foreman now does not discharge a worker. He gives him a "complaint memorandum." If this is disregarded he gives him a "suspension slip." This removes him from the pay-roll until reinstated by the labor department. This department acts at once. It either restores him "on probation," or orders a temporary lay-off or a discharge. The worker then has an appeal, if he wishes, to the "trade board." This is a shop committee of one workman and one foreman, presided over by a neutral chairman employed and paid equally by the company and the union. It gives a hearing, takes testimony, and may order reinstatement or modification of the penalty.

Finally, an ultimate appeal for either side lies to the "board of arbitration"—one person appointed by the company, one by the union, one by agreement of both parties. The "trade board" is the "trial court"—it gives the parties a hearing, investigates facts, takes testimony. The "board of arbitration" is the supreme court of the shop—it decides questions of law, interprets the constitution, *makes* the law.

The machinery seems complex. It would be complex if it had to act on every case of discipline. Autocracy is always more simple than democracy. It acts without consulting. Consultation takes time and acts according to rules. After this particular machinery got into working order many months have passed at times without an appeal to the high board of arbitration.

The reason is, "precedent." A case once decided is a rule of law for all succeeding cases. Like the Constitution of the United States, the agreement has become a "government of law and not of men." A man is not deprived of his job without "due process of law." This is the difference between democracy and autocracy, and the reason why the machinery of democracy is complex and that of autocracy is simple.

But when men learn to act according to law and precedent, then democracy also is simple enough. Its machinery is called in only when men are alleged to act contrary to the rule of law. Its strength resides in being ready to act and not needing to act.

This is the reason why democracy needs education. When this particular shop scheme was started, many of the workers were newly arrived immigrants, acquainted only with the despotisms of Austria, Hungary, Russia. Many were what is now known as bolshevistic, or revolutionary, socialists opposed to the wage system and believers in the immediate sovereignty of labor. Many were successful agitators, hostile to employers as a class. In course of time their employers were astonished at the change in

attitude that came over them. Misinformed, self-
seeking, unscrupulous leaders began to lose influence.
The other class of leaders came to the front, skilled
in negotiation, competent in pleadings and cross-
examinations before the trade boards, efficient and
firm in organizing, in leading and disciplining the
unruly among the workers. They have been learning
democracy and due process of law.

And the employers confess that they too have
learned. They had resented interference and limita-
tion of their authority. They wanted unrestricted
liberty. The machinery of consultation and discussion was vexatious. On innumerable occasions
they had to change their plans and policies against
their will.

But they learned that it was worth while to be
protected against themselves; that they needed to
make it impossible to violate or overlook the rights
of their employees. Especially they learned to approve of checks calculated to restrain their agents
from arbitrary and unjust acts toward fellow-em-
ployees. In short, what they think they have learned
is that, by admitting labor into the councils and
authority of the company, they are winning industrial
peace and the goodwill of labor.[1]

This is, indeed, a hard thing to learn for the business
man and engineer who has been accustomed to depend
upon his own judgment. The things that workers
deem important often seem so petty to him, who is
accustomed to large dealings, that to be compelled
to listen to their grievances is wholly vexatious.

[1] *The Hart, Shaffner and Marx Labor Agreement*, pamphlet published
by the company, Chicago, 1916.

I knew a highly competent specialist in office and factory management. He made a thorough investigation of the arrangement of desks and the routing of papers among the clerks in the offices of a certain large establishment, and then proceeded to rearrange the floor plan. The clerks came in to work one morning and found their desks shifted about. The man next to a good window was set over in a different corner. Another had his place. Instead of increasing the efficiency of that office the specialist had succeeded only in reducing it. He had not investigated *all* of the facts. He had thoroughly investigated the mechanical efficiency and the floor plan, but had not investigated the goodwill of the clerks. To him, the protests of an individual clerk who lost his good window were but a petty grouch.

But that clerk was part of a going concern. A code of procedure and a line of promotion had grown up in that office. To all of the clerks it was nearly as important to be promoted along the line from dark corners to good windows as to be promoted in salary or authority. They had learned to look forward to that promotion. Their devotion to present work had been built up largely on that expectancy. The goodwill of the whole office force had grown up on that floor plan. The specialist had investigated the floor plan but not the collective goodwill that went with it.

And how could he have investigated that goodwill except by collective negotiation with the entire force? If he accidentally heard the protest of one or two he might very well turn it down as a petty and selfish grouch. But had he consulted them all together through their committee freely chosen among themselves, he would have found that the grouch of one was the concern of all. · His scientific floor plan might have been delayed, would certainly have been changed, but in dozens of details he might have contrived to fit his expert judgment of mechanical efficiency into an equally expert judgment of spiritual efficiency. The one might be his own private judgment— the other his share in a collective judgment.

I do not know that this machinery of collective democracy can be successfully imposed by law where the employer or manager is unwilling. But willingness can be educated. Legislation is a crude and impersonal method of education. Willingness is a personal and every-day attitude of mind that sees the need and then does things before being compelled to do them. Often, however, willingness is preceded by a jolt. The present-day jolt is the freedom and unrest of labor. No capitalist more powerful has lived in America than John D. Rockefeller. While the Colorado Fuel and Iron Company, with the aid of the state government, was successfully resisting and overcoming the strike of the greatest labor organization in the country, the management called to their aid a leading authority on collective shop organization. They adopted and installed substantially all of the machinery of representative democracy above described that would have been adopted had the union been successful. The employees of each mining camp elect by secret ballot their representatives to act on their behalf in all matters pertaining to safety, health, housing, recreation, education, wages, hiring and firing. Rules of procedure, appeals from decisions of lower boards to higher boards—substantially all of the arrangements described above for a different establishment were adopted.   In order to guarantee good faith, the State Industrial Commission of Colorado is made the highest board of appeal in case of dispute between the company and the employees.   The rules protect the right of employees to organize by prohibiting any discrimination either by the company or its employees on account of membership or non-membership in any society, fraternity, or union.[1] After the apparently successful operation of this plan for a period of two years, the Rockefeller interests proceeded to install it in their refineries and properties elsewhere.[2]

The Rockefeller plan was adopted voluntarily, that is, without recognition of organized labor.   In this respect it is paternalistic rather than democratic. It is handed down rather than forced up.   One of the penalties of democracy is the cost of learning by experience.   And the history of democracy, whether in politics or industry, has been a history of costly experience in self-government.

Perhaps this is a necessary cost and inevitable. Many labor leaders think it is.   They prefer complete defeat and no organization at all, to a paternalistic union organized by the employer.   In some respects, this attitude is like that of revolutionary socialism. It is better to let conditions get as bad as possible because only then is revolution attractive to the oppressed.   Bolshevistic socialism is generally found

[1] Cf. *Industrial Representation Plan*, published by Colorado Fuel and Iron Company, Denver, Colorado (1915).

[2] See *Survey*, April 13, 1918.

in accord with reactionary capitalism, both of them standing firmly on their ultimate principles and natural rights, and both of them preventing the gradual introduction of democracy through half-way measures. The outcome is necessarily revolution and counter-revolution, revolt and reaction.

So with the history of labor organization. It has often been a long history of cycles of strikes and defeat, labor dictatorship alternating with employer dictatorship. But constitutional democracy in politics and industry has generally been procured by half-way measures. It may have its revolts, but generally they are anticipated by concessions in advance. The advance may not be great, but it stands, and is a starting point for a new advance. And this, because democracy must be built on education, good faith and goodwill. Education in self-government is slow. Good faith is experience of previous good faith. Goodwill is reciprocity. There is no conclusive reason why constitutional democracy may not start with the employer as with the employees. It depends on his good faith and goodwill. If he starts it as a subterfuge he is probably laying up trouble for himself and for others. If he starts it and continues it with recognition that as fast as possible the workers shall learn to govern themselves and to govern the shop in coöperation with himself,[1] then he is truly performing a public service for a nation which has admitted to its suffrage millions of voters unaccustomed to democracy.

Organization, whether it begins with the workers or with the employers, must always begin at the

[1] See Filene, E. A., "Why the Employees Run Our Business," *System*, December, 1918.

8

bottom, in the shop, rather than at the top by legislation or national organizations of capital and labor.
The national organizations of labor in England and
America began in the earlier days as shop unions.
Then these shop unions came together as local unions
in a town or district. It was not until railway transportation had brought shops and towns into competition that national unions arose in order to equalize
competitive conditions. At first, the national control
was weak. The national conventions were assemblies
of delegates from local sovereign unions. Gradually
the national union was granted increasing powers. It
took away from local unions their control over finances
and strikes. Then, in turn, it organized new local
unions, financed them, and conducted their strikes and
negotiations.

But, in all this cycle of shop, district, nation, and
back to district and shop, it is the shop, after all,
that constitutes the real unit of organization. It
may be effaced for a time; the local or district union
may dominate; control may be centralized at a distance, but it is in the shop that employer and employee
meet every day. It is there that trouble begins and
there that the real business of collective action goes
on. The national organization is the agent of the
shop organizations.

And, in the newly awakened spirit of collective
action, the employer, like the union, begins with his
own shop. If employers organize on a national scale
to contend with unionism, unions must parallel
their organization. If employers devote their attention to the real business of unionism, they attend to it
each in his own shop. It is here that their initiative,

originality, enterprise, personality, count. If they subject themselves to the dictates of a national association of employers they are likely to lose the chance to outrun their competitors in the new race for collective goodwill.

They may be compelled to submit to a national association of employers. That is one thing. But if they voluntarily submit to others then they abdicate the control of their own business at the very point where modern business is most delicately in the balance. Under the old system of competition and unregulated supply and demand, they might distance their competitors by cutting wages and driving labor, and, to protect themselves against the results of these practices they were often forced to join with their fellow-employers on a national scale. Under the new impulse of competitive goodwill, they naturally wish to be free from the control of the national labor unions. They cannot be free from that control if they submit to the control in their own shops of a national association of employers.

This is not saying that national associations, either of employers or of unions, have no place in the awakening new spirit of collective action. They have a place, but it is different. Their new place is more professional and educational, and less executive and governmental. It is the place for comparing notes and statistics, sharing experiences, telling each other of their successes and showing how it is done in dealing with labor. It is less and less the place for depriving the employer of his freedom to deal with his own employees in his own shop. Employers' associations will and must expand, but they should become great educational conferences on the methods, the purpose and the spirit of shop organization, rather than law-making bodies for their members.[1]

Likewise with national organizations of labor unions. The unparalleled solidity and executive power of the national unions in America, compared with organized labor in other countries, can be traced to the hostility of American employers and courts. With state protective legislation declared unconstitutional and with militant employers' associations, the natural line of development has been toward centralization of power in the hands of the national officers of a hundred or more national unions.[2]

Yet, while this very centralization was going on in the different unions, a great educational conference, with very little executive or legislative power over the constituent unions, has been enlarging its field. The authority of the American Federation of Labor is neither in its meagre financial power, nor in its control of strikes, but in its so-called "moral" assistance and its educational and professional conferences

---

[1] Possibly a beginning in this direction has been made in the National Industrial Conference Board, with its headquarters in Boston. See its publications on: *Workmen's Compensation Acts in the United States—The Legal Phase*, April, 1917; *Analysis of British Wartime Reports on Hours of Work as Related to Output and Fatigue*, November, 1917; *Strikes in American Industry in Wartime*, March, 1918; *Hours of Work as Related to Output and Health of Workers—Cotton Manufacturing*, March, 1918; *The Canadian Industrial Disputes Investigation Act*, April, 1918; *Sickness Insurance or Sickness Prevention?* May, 1918; *Hours of Work as Related to Output and Health of Workers— Boot and Shoe Industry*, June, 1918; *Wartime Employment of Women in the Metal Trades*, July, 1918; *Wartime Changes in Cost of Living*, October, 1918.

[2] Cf. Commons and Associates, *History of Labor in the United States*, I, 15; II, 42 *ff.*

of leaders and representatives from the constituent bodies. It is here that labor's policies are formulated, here the public opinion of labor is crystallized, and elsewhere these policies and opinions are adopted and executed in the shops.

Naturally enough it was this great educational conference of labor unions and the somewhat similar National Industrial Conference Board of employers' associations which were called upon by President Wilson to create the National War Labor Board.[1]

For it was the crisis of war that gave national importance both to the educational work of the national organizations of capital and labor and to the daily and hourly activities in the shops. The war weakened, at least for a time, the executive and legislative control of the national labor unions over the shop unions, for it took away from national unions the right to authorize, finance and support strikes.

In England this was done by legislation which made it a legal offense to interfere with production.[2] In America it was no less effectively done by the voluntary consent of the national leaders.

Yet while law or public opinion can reach the small number of national leaders, or can tie up the funds of the unions, it cannot reach the hundreds and thousands who go out spontaneously in a mass on strike. Illegal or unauthorized local strikes in England forced the government to waive the penalties of the

[1] See Documents of National War Labor Board; *Proclamation by the President of the United States* (April 8, 1918); *Official Bulletin,* April 10, 1918, p. 3.

[2] *Munitions of War Act,* July 2, 1915; *Defence of the Realm Act,* August 8, 1914; August 28, 1914; November 27, 1914.

law, to go over the heads of the national leaders, and to negotiate directly with the strikers. It could not even enforce legal penalties on the local leaders, for that but shifted the demands of the strike from the correction of shop grievances to the release of the leaders. These leaders were simply the "works committees" or the "shop stewards" so-called, selected from among the workers by their fellow-workers, to represent them in negotiations with employers. Protected by this immunity the shop committees, rather than the national unions, became the spokesmen of unrest, and the main result of legislation prohibiting strikes was to shift negotiations from headquarters into the shops. Compulsion failed, and the government after two and a half years' experiment with compulsory methods, proceeded to recommend and introduce more nearly voluntary methods into the shops and localities.

Since the object was to *prevent* shop friction rather than to remedy it after it became acute, the government not only recognized the "works committee" system where organized labor had already installed it, but extended it to factories where there was no trade-union organization. Hence by pressure and recommendation rather than legal penalties, the shops of England have become organized more or less into joint committees of employers and employees for the purpose of dealing with their shop problems. The details of these organizations are widely different, according to previous conditions, but the underlying principle is the freedom of employees in each shop to be represented collectively by committees of their own choosing, and the duty of their employers to deal collectively with these committees in their own shops. National or district organization, so-called "joint standing industrial councils," representing national unions if such existed, were recommended for the purpose of agreeing on standards that might equalize conditions, but these standards were to be only recommendations to the several "works committees."[1]

In America a similar policy was adopted after the first year of war, but without the intervening experiment of legislation prohibiting strikes. The National War Labor Board, representing in equal numbers the American Federation of Labor and the National Industrial Conference Board, issued its statement of policy to be followed whenever called upon to decide a dispute. This policy asserted the right of both workers and employers to organize in trade unions and associations and to bargain collectively through chosen representatives; and it prohibited either side from discriminations or coercion in the maintenance of the right to organize.

Instead, however, of providing for joint standing industrial councils in the several industries, as was done in England, the National War Labor Board

[1] First Whitley Report, *Interim Report on Joint Standing Industrial Councils*, March 8, 1917, Cd. 8606; Second Whitley Report, *Second Report on Joint Standing Industrial Councils*, October 18, 1917, Cd. 9002; Third Report, *Supplementary Report on Works Committees*, October 18, 1917, Cd. 9001; Fourth Report, *Industrial Reports, Number 2*, March, 1918; Fifth Report, *Fifth and Final Report of the Whitley Committee*, September 18, 1918. See also *Monthly Review*, Bureau of Labor Statistics, September, 1917, pp. 130–132; October, 1917, pp. 33–38; March, 1918, pp. 81–84; May, 1918, pp. 59–61; June, 1918, pp. 27, 28; August, 1918, pp. 76–79, 80, 81–84, 237–240; September, 1918, pp. 53–58.

reserved to itself a direct appeal from each shop, and the appointment of its own members or agents to take evidence where an appeal was made. The provisions against discriminations and the appeals to the outside board, render the system substantially the same in its principles as those already described in the early pages of this chapter.[1]

During the war a certain degree of compulsion gave sanction to these policies and decisions of the National War Labor Board, for the President was given authority to take over the property of an employer as well as to make rules for drafting workers into the army or assigning them to industries through the federal employment offices. His prompt use of this authority where the decisions of the National War Labor Board were disregarded, added, of course, an indirect compulsion to their decisions. Even so, it is doubtful whether it has been his threat of compulsion or his appeal to patriotism that has prevented strikes.

In the face of necessary long delays in reaching decisions by the National Board the enduring success of the Board must turn on the successful working of the shop committees and shop organizations. These cannot always be expected to agree, and some provision for appeal must be made. It gets back again

[1] See documents of the National War Labor Board, 1918, as follows: *Proclamation by the President of the United States* (April 8, 1918); *Functions, Powers and Duties of the Board; Principles and Policies to Govern Relations Between Workers and Employers; Method of Presenting Complaints and Procedure of Board*. Also *Official Bulletin*, April 10, 1918, p. 3.

[2] *Official Bulletin*, June 4, 1918, p. 6; September 4, 1918, p. 8; September 18, 1918, p. 1. *Docket* 132, National War Labor Board; *Docket* 273, National War Labor Board.

to the spirit of democracy. Superior authority, for a time, may install and impose the machinery of democracy, but, if the spirit is lacking the machinery clogs. And in time of peace, even the machinery cannot be imposed on a large scale without consequences more serious in other directions.[1]

The shop-committee system has been installed, and may be installed by employers as a mere subterfuge, designed to ward off a real shop organization by controlling the elections of its committees, by mixing unorganized with organized workers, by preventing the employment of trade unionists. The committee may have only a nominal existence and its recommendations be disregarded by the management. It may be permitted to deal only with social and athletic activities. It may go further and deal with accident and sickness prevention, mutual benefits and insurance. These are, indeed, important and a necessary beginning. They deal with non-controversial questions, where there is no ultimate clash of interests, since the disputes arise over methods to be adopted for reaching an object already agreed upon. The critical question is whether they are permitted to go forward into the truly bargaining activities which decide the ultimate clash of interests—whether they take part in fixing wage and piece-rates, time and speed standards, apprenticeship and training, introduction of new processes, substitutions, transfers and promotions, the execution of standards nationally agreed upon. On these points is the test.

Probably in no shop should a single committee deal with these several kinds of industrial problems.

[1] Below, Chapter XVI, *Depression.*

Social clubs and athletics are one thing; safety, sickness benefits and insurance are another; wages, output, discipline, are a third and very different. The qualities and training, and above all the personality needed for one are different from those needed in the other.[1] And the suitable personality on the part of the employer's representatives is just as difficult to obtain as it is on the part of the workers' representatives.

The machinery which I have described at the beginning of this chapter could not have been developed were it not that, back of it, on the part of the employer's representatives, was the patience, the self-control, the ability to listen to error as well as reason, the willingness to submit to rules regularly adopted even though vexatious and mistaken, in short, the personality that constitutes the spirit of reasonableness.

And we know that organized labor is as likely to be arbitrary as the employer if it has the power, and its spokesmen can be as ingenious and plausible in justifying it. In the name of democracy labor may be as despotic as capital in the name of liberty.

Democracy is conservative. At all times in the world's history the less privileged classes appeal instinctively to custom as their protection against arbitrary power. Whatever is customary is familiar and safe. Innovation is a menace, a threat, a hardship. The laborer instinctively opposes machinery. When I told a cotton-mill operative that an automatic loom had been invented by which one weaver

[1] An interesting analysis of these different problems and corresponding committees is made by C. G. Renold, Manchester, England, reprinted in America by the *Survey*, Supplement, October 5, 1918.

could operate twenty-four looms, he promptly said the inventor ought to be shot.

Liberty is progressive. It breaks down custom. How shall the two be brought together? Capital has had its nineteenth century of unrestricted liberty. It has broken down custom. Must it break down democracy because democracy is conservative?

The labor unions of the country secured legislation by Congress which prevents the government arsenals and navy yards from employing any methods of time and motion studies, of stop-watch or measuring devices designed to ascertain the speed at which the laborer can work.[1] Certain unions seem to have made it an unnegotiable demand in their proposed agreements with employers. This is the obstructive answer of organized labor to the unrestricted liberty of capital.

But accurate methods of measurement are as necessary for industrial democracy as they are for the progress of industry. Before the "trade board" machinery, described at the beginning of this chapter, was in working order, the piece-rates were made by the foreman. He made and unmade the rates and changed them at will. After three or four years' experience the following regulation was evolved:

"Whenever a change of piece-rate is contemplated the matter shall be referred to a specially appointed rate committee who shall fix the rate according to the change of work. If the committee disagree the Trade Board shall fix the rate. In fixing the rates, the Board is restricted to the following rule:

"Changed rates must correspond to the changed work and new rates must be based upon old rates where possible."

[1] *United States Statutes At Large*, Vol. 39, Part I, 64th Cong. I Sess. (1916), Ch. 417; 64th Cong. II Sess. (1917), Ch. 180.

In practice it works out as follows: The two representatives on the Trade Board constitute themselves a committee of time-and-motion study experts in order to fix the prices of work. These work together with their stop-watch, if needed, to ascertain and agree upon the time required to make the new piece, and to calculate the corresponding piece-rate required to make the standard wage. Of course, they do not stand over the workers and make time studies of all workers while at work. The study is made of selected workers in an experimental laboratory, and is made, not to speed up the workers, but to agree on a piece-rate. The decision is made by the neutral chairman, and the new rates are always provisional and temporary.

Thus does the machinery of shop committees adjust itself to the scientific study of efficiency. The notion is dispelled that a stop-watch is scientific only when placed in the hands of a disinterested outsider. There are dozens of factors that cannot be measured by a watch. The selection of the operative whose motions are timed is a matter of opinion as to whether he is representative of the general run of workers. Whether he pulls out or holds back is a matter of opinion. Whether he encumbers himself with wasteful motions is largely a matter of opinion. On these and other points opinions differ. And the workers are just as much concerned as the management to have the measurements accurate. For their wages and speed depend upon it. Where opinions differ there can be no accuracy, in the mechanical sense, but there may be conciliation and a working agreement. It all depends on that spirit of democracy which is patience and willingness to listen and act according to that due process of law wherein all the facts are considered and due weight is given to each. And this depends just as much on labor's reasonableness as on employers' reasonableness.

Thus shop organization is the focus of all problems of employment. Politics, legislation, national associations of capital and labor, all else are outside and overhead. They affect the shop somewhat, but it is the shop conditions and the attitude in the shops of the nation that tell what the nation shall be. There is where, more than ever before, the nation's life is maintained in war and peace. In the first year of the world's war Germany fired five or six explosive shells to every one fired by England and France. In the last year of the war England and France fired five or six to Germany's one. When the American boys stopped the Germans at the Marne it was because ammunition flowed to them like a river. It was shop organization that won the war. Capital and labor, for the time, laid down their industrial war and united in the shop as Allies. The lesson of war is the lesson for peace. Since the war is won shall the shops return to war? Rather shall they not make more perfect that willingness to listen, that patience with the faults of others, that procedure that consults first and acts afterward, which constitutes the spirit and substance of democracy? And shall they not, in peace as in war, combine loyalty to the nation with loyalty to each other?

XIII

EDUCATION

In Pittsburgh I found the minimum value of the English language was 2 cents an hour. Non-English-speaking immigrants were getting 15½ cents an hour, and English-speaking immigrants doing similar work were getting 17½ cents an hour.

Of the 9,500,000 young men registered for the first selective draft, 1,200,000 were citizens of foreign countries and could not be required to serve in the American armies.[1] Working side by side in our factories and on our farms, 8,000,000 American citizens could be drafted to offer their lives in behalf of the prosperity and high wages of 1,000,000 privileged immigrants free to remain at work.

The state of Arizona enacted a law to the effect that employers in that state should employ at least 80 per cent of their force who were citizens and only 20 per cent who were not citizens. The Supreme Court of the United States declared the law unconstitutional on the ground that every person in America, citizen or alien, has a right to work in American industries.[2]

Such is the outcome of a theory that goes back to the Declaration of Independence and asserts the

---

[1] *Report of the Provost Marshal General to the Secretary of War, on the First Draft under the Selective-Service Act,* 1917 (1918), pp. 53–56, 86, 87.

[2] Truax v. Raich, 239 U. S. 33 (1915).

natural and inalienable rights of man, without assert-
ing the accompanying principle that every right has
its reciprocal duty. The immigrant has a natural
right to work and the employer has a natural right to
employ him, but the immigrant has no reciprocal
duty to serve the nation that gives him liberty and
the employer no reciprocal duty to educate or
Americanize him.

Thirty years ago the state of Wisconsin placed on
its statute books a law requiring private and parochial
schools to give a minimum amount of instruction
in the English language and to be subject to the
inspection of the State Superintendent of Schools similar to that of public schools.[1]   On the plea of liberty
and freedom of worship the law was soon repealed,
and those who sought freedom in America have been
free of this particular duty to become American.

The eighteenth and nineteenth centuries were centuries of struggle against autocracy and slavery.
The theory of natural and inalienable rights of man
served its purpose in the French and American
Revolutions and the American Civil War. Kings
and slaves disappeared.

But the results were negative. The twentieth
century will determine the kind of democracy or
even autocracy that will take the place of the old.
A theory of reciprocal and inalienable *duties* of man
is needed to determine positively the results of the
World War.

The employer who hires immigrant labor is hiring
cheap labor with low standards of living and ignorance
of self-government.   They are one of his weapons

[1] *Wisconsin Statutes*, 1889, Chapter 519.

to restrain American labor from obtaining high wages and supporting a high standard of living. The immigrant who works eight hours a day and earns two or three times as much as he earned in Europe for twelve hours, is reaping the harvest of liberty and plenty which American labor and American democracy have won for him.

The employer, or immigrant, or justice of a Supreme Court, who fails to look for any reciprocal duty attaching to this enjoyment of power, liberty and prosperity, is living in the past and fighting an autocracy that has ceased to exist. The new autocracy that is arising on the ruins of the old is economic rather than political, and it arises because it asserts rights of liberty and property that have already been won, and evades duties to the democracy that has won them.

Duties subtract from rights. It costs something to fulfill duties. How heavy the duties shall be made in consideration of the rights is a matter of good judgment under the circumstances, of willingness to do one's share, of patriotism. In ordinary business the law of demand and supply compels the employer to pay producers the full cost of getting out the raw material which he buys. The price that he pays for coal, iron, lumber, wheat, cotton, covers not only the cost of furnishing the material but also the cost of depreciation, the costs of risks, the cost of keeping up the fertility of the soil, or the cost of developing additional sources of raw material to take the place of that which is being depleted. He pays for conservation of the resources from which his raw material is derived, else the supply would not continue to be forthcoming.

Somebody must pay for the conservation of the nation's human resources. If left to demand and supply, the most valuable resources are not conserved. For labor is both the source of demand for products and the source of supply of the same products. A nation of sick, ignorant, or rebellious workers produces enough products to keep them sick, ignorant, and unpatriotic. Demand-and-supply goes in a circle when the thing demanded is the supply of health, intelligence and the qualities of citizenship.

We have learned to compel parents to send their children to school and to compel tax-payers to pay for their schooling, even though the parent has no desire for it and the tax-payer no children. It is their duty to set aside the law of demand and supply of school teachers.

We have learned somewhat to enforce the duty of taking care of health where the menace is contagious or infectious, and the duty of tax-payers to pay the bills even though they do not demand the services of physicians, nurses and hospitals for others beside themselves.

We have been thinking somewhat of the duties of citizenship and have seen the injustice of compelling some to offer their lives for the good of others who claim allegiance to other nations, or no nation. Duties are as inalienable as rights. The problem of democracy is how to distribute duties as well as rights.

Employers control one-half to two-thirds of the working hours of labor. Without this control they

9

cannot make profits. They convert the nation's human resources, like its natural resources, into products, and meanwhile they take their share.

These human resources come to them after a heavy investment. The parents have invested something. The tax-payers and the schools have invested something. Many children and youths have been lost on the way but not charged off. The nation invests several hundred—possibly several thousand—dollars, unaccounted for and uncredited in every worker who reaches the age of production. And many workers come from foreign lands where much less has been invested in bringing them up.

The employer of immigrant labor is paying less than the full cost of production of American labor. And the immigrant laborer is getting excess profits on the investment that has been put into him.

That the employer should be required to send the immigrant to school and the immigrant be required to attend school in the day time on the employer's time is but a duty that each may justly owe to the preservation of the nation that enriches them both.

That the immigrant should become American and that his employer should give thought and money and leadership to bring to him an understanding and love of America is but a small compensation for what America does for them.

And no person is in such an advantageous position as the employer. He controls the immigrant's time and livelihood; he sets the example by which the immigrant gets an idea of what American democracy means. How baffling was the experience of a member of the American Labor Mission sent to Europe to win the workers away from the socialist propaganda of Germany, when he was met by the retort of returned Italian workers that America had ruined their health and exploited their labor.

Like other duties the duty of education cannot in fairness be borne by individual employers unless their competitors carry a similar burden. If one employer teaches English to his immigrants and others do not, the others bid up the price and the public-spirited one loses his investment. The associated employers of Detroit, Cleveland, and other cities have begun to bring pressure on their fellow employers to teach English. I knew a corporation that started a school for apprentices. After spending considerable money on their education, as soon as the apprentices reached the point where they could return something on the investment, and even before their education was completed, other employers began to steal them by offering higher wages.

American industry needs schools for apprentices. These schools must be in the shops and the apprentices must get a living wage while learning. When the tax-payers set up separate trade schools, only a very few boys are financially able to attend, and they are trained for only the small number of trades that have not yet been broken up by machinery. The state of Wisconsin attempts to get all employers to take on apprentices, by enforcing apprenticeship contracts, so that the boy may get an all-round training, may be paid while learning, and be prevented from leaving before his training is finished. But the contracts themselves are voluntary. No employer is compelled to take apprentices and no boy or parent is compelled to sign a contract. Furthermore, public opinion does not seem to support prosecutions for enforcement of the contracts although the law imposes penalties on the employer for violations and on the boy for running away.[1] The law is advantageous but not universal. Like the separate trade school it is limited by the small number of employers and the small number of trades. Consequently, it merges into the continuation school, which is universal apprenticeship.

About two-thirds of the boys and girls who enter school drop out at the end of the compulsory attendance period, and nine-tenths of them drop out before completing the four-year high school.[2] Their industrial education then begins. The employer is their school master. For many of them, attendance is compulsory, for they must earn a living for themselves and parents. The employer is conducting a compulsory private school for the nation's future workers. His fees are the profits he can make on the work of his pupils. His school is as important as the public schools in the scheme of compulsory education. In the public schools, the child does not and should not learn to be a worker. Then is the time for play. Yet to learn to work and to be interested in work is the sure foundation for advancement and citizenship.

Unfortunately, the employers generally have acquired a bad reputation in the conduct of their schools. They have been notorious in defending their right to the fees and avoiding their duty to furnish the

[1] *Wisconsin Laws* (1915), Chapter 133, Section 2377.
[2] Inglis, Alexander, *Principles of Secondary Education* (1918), p. 125.

education. For a hundred years in Europe and
America they have resisted efforts to take away from
them their power over the child. Even employers
who know better and who strive to be models in their
own establishments have been found to line themselves up with competitors whose reputation is bad. In
this respect even the best of them have earned the
stigma of acting together as a class against the public
interest, instead of endeavoring to lift their competitors to the higher level of meeting their obligations.

And so, when it comes to the continuation schools,
and the nation proceeds positively to require employers to devote five, six, or eight hours a week to the
education of their pupils as workers, many people
are loath to trust them with even a voice in the management of their schools. And this is true, notwithstanding the cordial and sincere endorsement of the
compulsory part-time schools by leaders among the
manufacturers.[1]

Yet, who is there more fitted by his own training
and daily experience to have a voice in the management of these schools? The employers, or at least
their managers, have come up through the shop.
They have learned by hard knocks just those little

[1] National Association of Manufacturers: "We favor the establishment in every community of continuation schools wherein the children
of fourteen to eighteen years of age, now in the industries, shall be
instructed in the science and art of their respective industries and in
citizenship." "It is the right of every one of these children to be given
an education that will make him efficient and reasonably happy, able
properly to maintain himself and meet the various obligations of life
and citizenship." "A nation cannot live half slave and half free,
half educated and half uneducated. God help the man whose vision
is not clear enough to see that the employers see this." *Proceedings
of Annual Conventions*, 1911; 1912, p. 150; 1913, p. 238.

turning points that are met every day and lead to success or failure. They are in daily contact with wage-earners and they know the qualities that get the workers their promotions and the qualities that keep them back.

The school teacher in the public schools or the high schools, or colleges or universities, cannot really know these details that fit the workers for promotion in industry. They can teach what they know but not what they do not know. When they are in control of industrial education they run it into arts, or crafts, or manual training, or mechanical exercises, or something that does not connect up with the shop as it actually is in modern industry.

Yet they stand for what employers as a class do not stand for. They stand for education and citizenship, and not for the fees and profits. No wonder that in the distrust of employers the school teacher is listened to and often is given control where he is not fitted to control.

And especially is the wage-earner bewildered by this clash of school teacher and employer for control. He knows that the school teacher does not fit his children into industry and he distrusts the employers,[1]

[1] American Federation of Labor: "If we permit the present academic educational group of the nation to dominate, the whole force and virtue of genuine vocational trade training will be in danger of being lost sight of and the nation's appropriations will probably be misdirected along minor lines of endeavor, such as manual training, amateur mechanics and other trifling, impractical valueless schemes. Neither can we afford to permit this great measure to be over-weighted by any special trade, commercial or vocational interests. The agriculturists should not predominate, neither should the commercial or even the labor and industrial interests." *Report of Proceedings*, 1916, p. 103.

particularly in these days when the educator can invoke the dread of "prussianizing" and "commercializing" the continuation schools.[1]

Undoubtedly, the idea of compulsory part-time school is German in its origin. It was first adopted by imperial legislation more than twenty years ago.[2] But it may be made American in its management. If the employers alone are in control, it might be "commercialized." If the school teacher alone controls, it loses contact with the shop. If the wage-earner alone controls, it might be used to restrict apprenticeship. Joint control is democratic control. It enlists the qualities of each that are needed, and checks the defects of each.

The Federal Vocational Education Law of 1917 attempts to establish this joint control.[3] It attempts to give representation to the employer, the educator, the wage-earner. It attempts to secure similar joint control in the states and in the local continuation

---

[1] "What do I mean by Prussianizing our education? I mean primarily this: (1) a subtle, even if unconscious, attempt to use the children of the laboring people, including farmers, as cogs in a machine; an attempt to follow the lead of the caste system in Germany, a system which defrauds children of an opportunity for secondary education and practically dooms nine-tenths of the people to be and to remain hewers of wood and drawers of water; (2) a division of the school system into two parts, each striving for financial support and developing rivalries of a pernicious kind. It should be noted that in Prussia there is no rivalry between the two systems, for everybody who counts concedes that when the children of the common people finish the common school there is nothing more for them but toil and the army." Superintendent of Public Instruction, Wisconsin. *Educational News Bulletin*, November 1, 1918, p. 3.

[2] Hoffman, *Die Gewerbe-Ordnung*, Section 120.

[3] Smith-Hughes Act, approved February 23, 1917. See *Vocational Summary*, published monthly by Federal Board for Vocational Education, beginning May, 1918.

schools. It attempts to eliminate autocracy, either of employers, pedagogues, or wage-earners. It attempts to secure representative democracy in education. If this scheme of representative control succeeds, how great are its possibilities! It is universal, industrial, educational.

The public grade schools give universal education, but not industrial, and they should not. Theirs is the all-round preparation for any and every position. It is play, not work. But education cannot stop at fourteen, or sixteen, or even twenty-one years of age. If it stops, then there is no future, for the future is advancement, and advancement stops when learning stops. The high school, the college, the university, the technical school, leads on to certain specialized professions, increasing in number but always limited, for they are not self-supporting. They feed on industry and thrive only as industry thrives. It is in agriculture, manufactures, transportation, merchandizing, business, that the nation lives and the millions find promotion. To open up the lines of advancement in industry according to the aptitudes and abilities of every individual is the aim of industrial democracy. The trade school cannot do it. The apprenticeship school cannot do it. They are limited to the skilled trades. The public schools cannot do it. They are not industrial. Only universal apprenticeship can do it, where the common laborer, the unskilled worker, the immigrant and the children of the entire nation shall have equal opportunities in both education and industry.

And universal apprenticeship is but the compulsory continuation or part-time school. It may be four, eight, or more hours a week, or even half-time, according as experience and good judgment advise. It may extend to the age of sixteen, then to eighteen, according as the instruction is found practicable and the teachers competent. It may extend still further for immigrants who have not learned the English language.

To be universal it must be compulsory, in the day time and on the employer's time. The tired worker in night school is not a learner. Attendance there is neither compulsory, universal, nor fruitful. Only on the employer's time, when the learner must attend in order to earn his living, can attendance be universal and instruction educational.

The first great awakening of England aroused by the war is this union of education and industry. No nation ever suffered more from the exploitation of children in factories. And England led the world in excluding young children from factories. But education stopped where industry began. Two-fifths of the boys and girls between the ages of twelve and sixteen receive no further education after the age of thirteen. "These figures," said a group of British employers and trade unionists, "make it easy to understand the superior success of Germany in so many departments of activity. That success . . . is due to the fact that so very much greater a proportion of young people in that country receive any systematic education at all during the all-important years between fourteen and eighteen."[1] On the strength of

[1] *Memorandum on the Industrial Situation after the War*, Garton Foundation, Section 97 (1917). Reprint by United States Shipping Board, Emergency Fleet Corporation (1918).

these facts the British Parliament enacted the law of August, 1918, looking toward the continuation school.

In America, conditions are similar. Probably a million boys and girls leave school annually from grades above the sixth grade, and nine-tenths of the total number of children enter various occupations before eighteen years of age.[1] The Vocational Education Law of 1917 is America's awakening to this gap between industry and education.

Rights have their reciprocal duties. Duties, in the long run, are duties to the nation that grants and protects the rights. But duties cannot be left to autocrats or bureaucrats, or to a single class to impose on other classes. Germany set the example of enforcing duties on employers and parents to provide universal education. If Germany's system is faulty it is not on account of the recognition of universal duties but on account of autocratic or bureaucratic control in enforcing the duties. A wrong direction may be given to a good thing. Chemistry acts much the same in Germany as in America, but the German government may use it for different purposes. Modern industry is no respecter of nations, and the psychology of boys and girls is about the same in Europe as in America. But one nation may direct it toward conquest or obedience or the supremacy of one class over other classes; another nation may direct it toward democracy and equal opportunity for advancement to every person in every class. It depends on the control.

[1] Inglis, Alexander, *Principles of Secondary Education* (1918), pp. 575, 576.

No class can be trusted to decide for itself. No class, either aristocrats, capitalists, educators or workers, can see the needs, or rights, or duties, of others as vividly as its own. Democracy in education, like democracy in politics or industry, is not a philosophy or a theory or even a "science" of education—it is joint control over the teachers.

The modern advanced philosophy of education is fully awake to the vocational needs of education. It is fully aware that these needs cannot be met while teachers adhere to their "traditional ideals of culture, traditional subjects of study and traditional methods of teaching and discipline."[1] But these advanced ideas are not and cannot be generally put into practice while school teachers remain in bureaucratic control; for, like other experts, if uncontrolled they followed the traditions of bureaucracy rather than the science of education. When the teachers are jointly controlled, when organized teachers, organized employers and organized labor have each an equal voice in the control, when democracy in education is truly representative democracy, then the teachers begin to see the connections of education and industry, and to modify their traditional methods according to both the needs of industry and the philosophy of education.

For the business of the vocational teacher is to make industry interesting. Very few laborers can reach the top. On this account some people despair of ever making work interesting. They feel that,

[1] Dewey, John, *Democracy and Education* (1915), p. 114. See also Inglis, Alexander, *Principles of Secondary Education* (1918), pp. 572–620; Miller, H. L., "Adequate Schooling for the Youth of the Nation," *Inter-Mountain Educator*, September, October, 1918.

since the workers are compelled to settle down in grooves, industry can have no meaning or incentive for them. If this conclusion is true, then the situation is hopeless. For, as far as we can see, the forces of steam, electricity, transportation, are driving industry into large concerns. Twenty thousand men in one factory can make automobiles cheaper than one thousand. Room at the top is lessening and the number of workers tied into grooves is increasing.

The outlook is menacing for the worker, for industry, for the nation. The workers lose their interest in industry just at the time when they become more powerful than ever before in controlling industry through labor organization or politics. Without interest in their work they cannot be expected to pay attention or have a care for the economy, efficiency, or discipline, without which business goes bankrupt.

The inventors, the engineers, the business men, have brought on this situation. They have mastered the forces of nature and will increase their mastery. They have converted nature into capital and labor into an army. The problem of capital is the physical sciences—chemistry, electricity, physics, biology. The problem of labor is the human science, psychology. If it is the engineer who is the expert in physical science, it is the educator who becomes expert in psychology. The future of industry is psychological. The inventors, engineers, business men of the future will be industrial psychologists. Industry must be educational, and it is this very problem of opening up lines of promotion where physical science has closed them that is the problem of industrial education.

For interest in one's work does not depend on a

remote expectation of reaching the top. It is the *next step* that is interesting. The next step means accomplishment, means overcoming obstacles that are not hopeless, means initiative, means thinking on the job.[1] To the mere "intellectual" who ponders over the labor problem, there is no hope if there is no room at the top. Hence efforts to interest workers even in the next step are despaired of. To the business man and engineer whose opinions are formed in mastering the physical sciences, the worker is often preferred who does not think or talk back. But to the educator it is these very qualities which others reject that are his problem to be worked out. They are the psychological problems of industry. If industry has lessened the chances of promotion it is the educator's business to open them up again. He must work out lines of advancement that may serve as a substitute at least for the lost chances of promotion. He must know how to suggest these lines of advancement to the employer and the worker and to work them out practically. If he sees workers confined to "enervating" jobs he must know how to get them "energized."[2] And, just as the business man has employed and made use in the past of the inventor or engineer who reduces the physical sciences to practice, so must he enlist the inventive educator in making his business educational.

[1] Cf. Dewey, John, *Democracy and Education*, pp. 146–162; Marot, Helen, *Creative Impulse in Industry* (1918); Commons, *Labor and Administration*, pp. 363–381.

[2] Cf. Schneider, Herman, *Report on Public School System, New York Board of Estimate and Apportionment*, 1911–12, Part II, pp. 765–773. *Education for Industrial Workers*, World Book Company New York, 1915.

Then may we expect that industrial education will take its proper place. Schools and industry will dove-tail. Neither employer, laborer, nor educator will dominate. The educator will come out from his seclusion and will become industrial without being commercialized, for he will bring to industry the science of psychology. Business will become educational without being academic, for it will have its daily problems of education which cannot wait for a remote future. And labor will become more generally interested in the work, in addition to the compensation.

XIV

LOYALTY

Lack of interest and lack of loyalty are frequent complaints respecting the modern laborer. The complaint comes from different sides. Some people are hardened to it and expect it. With them lack of interest or loyalty is a kind of original sin. There is no remedy for it except to lay down the law of hiring and firing, with its penalty of unemployment.

At the other extreme are the doctrinaire socialists and anarchists. Man is born, as it were, with an instinct of workmanship, and coercion crushes it out of him. Abolish private property with its right to hire and fire and its penalty of unemployment and then you will "liberate" this suppressed instinct.

One extreme provokes the other. If there were only the theories of original depravity and original perfectibility, there would be no outcome but revolution and counter-revolution.

The problem is statistical. The wage system *is* compulsory, but it is also persuasive. It rewards *and* punishes. We could hardly expect that some kinds of work or some kinds of employers would ever inspire interest or loyalty; or that some kinds of laborers would ever get interested or loyal. The wage system with them is compulsory and penal. Other kinds of work are interesting, other employers are inspiring, other workers improvable. With them the wage system is persuasive and energizing. There are as many possible remedies for disloyalty and indifference as there are differences in employers, workers and kinds of work.

A mediæval and romantic remedy goes back to the time when the skilled worker did all parts of the work and made a finished job from raw material to artistic product.[1]

But how small was the number of skilled workers compared with the number of all the workers! There is probably a larger proportion of highly skilled workers and highly interesting work in modern industry than there was in the mediæval system, if we take into account all the work from raw material to finished product.

Besides, suppose the arts and crafts movement should succeed and should enable the worker again to make his all-round finished product. If there were very many of them they would need to sell their products in distant markets, and immediately the factory system would start up again with its artistic designers, its division of labor into skilled, semi-skilled and unskilled, its big employers, its wholesalers, jobbers, and distant retailers.

Or, suppose that trade unions of skilled workers should succeed, as some have done for a time, in preventing specialization and subdivision of labor, in order that they might retain their all-round proficiency. If their product is shipped to distant markets, or their partly finished work can be done

[1] Morris, William, *Art and Socialism* (1884); *A Dream of John Ball* (1888).

near the source of raw material, then factories will start up and eat into their jurisdiction.

Arts, crafts, and unions, in time, have yielded and must yield to the specialization imposed by transportation and large establishments. The worker's interest and loyalty, if it is aroused, must be his interest in a joint product and his loyalty to a going concern.

A certain establishment takes its younger applicants for employment on a trip throughout the plant before setting them at work on their own specialty. The different processes are pointed out, partly explained, and the finished product is exhibited. The systems of payment are explained, the chances for promotion, responsibility, and outlook are canvassed. Then the applicant is asked to come back the next day, after talking and thinking it over. If hired, then a daily follow-up ensues until the beginner gets acquainted with the work and with other workers and feels at home. Immediately, in that establishment, after starting this practice, the expensive turnover of the first week or month of employment and its resulting breakage of material, was reduced to almost negligible quantities. Two things are believed to be accomplished. A narrow specialized job is seen as an essential part of a marvellous system, and the fellow-workers and management are seen to be looking for steady workers and good companions. A beginning is made in the spirit of workmanship and loyalty to the business.

In another establishment a school is started for all beginners. At first, skilled operatives were put in as teachers. They knew how to do the work but not

10

how to teach it. They did the work themselves, told the beginner to look on and then imitate. Eventually a school teacher was employed, and the skilled operatives were sent back to their machines. The teacher did not ask the beginners to look on and imitate, but asked them to study out the machine, to study their own motions, to study the whys and purposes. The company pays them wages during this period of studying. A beginning is made in interest and loyalty—in interest, because there is something to think about; in loyalty, because somebody has given them a little taste of real thinking and mental advancement. That establishment has a supply of competent beginners when its competitors are short-handed.

A worker on repetition work was telling how he kept himself from going crazy. When he went to work in the morning he would start up a line of imagination, picturing himself perhaps as a prince, going through a day of romance, adventure, combat, heroism, love; or a line of reminiscence going over the events of his childhood or of the night before. He kept his mind away from his work.

In a public employment office I found that a large proportion of the applicants for work were boys or young men on these repetition jobs in machine shops. They had been on one machine for a month, or two months, or six months, and just wanted a change— a different machine or even the same machine in a different shop. But there were no middle-aged men in this class of applicants. The older men had lost their hankering for a change, had gotten used to monotony, or had quit for good.

Repetition work must be done by somebody. A foreman told me he wanted fairly stupid peasant women from Europe and did not want them to think. There ought to be a place in industry for all kinds of people. It is too bad that, just because a person cannot think, he cannot find a job. But, somehow, when one sees how ingenious, inventive, and enterprising employers are at all points where they can make money by improvements, one cannot help wishing that it could be made unprofitable to keep any worker on this kind of merely repetition work. The kind of work creates its own supply of the kind of labor suited to it. Perhaps, if the laborer's minimum wages were materially increased or his hours materially shortened, employers would substitute automatic or semi-automatic machinery. A worker attending a dozen machines has far more interesting work than one who is feeding a single machine. And when the whole factory gets automatic and the work comes along on trolleys and conveyors, a thousand men and boys strung along in a team have a more interesting time than the same number working by themselves. Their work is, indeed, repetition work, and each one adds but his own little specialized motion to the total, but it is sociable and democratic. Instead of a few skilled workers each making an all-round product, hundreds and thousands of unskilled get into the game. The great automatic modern factory has probably more chances for interesting work for more people than ever did the medieval and romantic small shop.

Repetition work seems to be a transition stage from handwork to automatic work. The automatic machine and factory may cost more money and require a larger investment and a larger factory. As long as wages are low and hours long it may be cheaper to keep the repetition process. When wages go up and hours go down then it may be cheaper to bring in the more nearly automatic process.

Yet it would be foolish to suggest any one panacea for uninteresting work. How to make work interesting is just as much a field of investigation and experiment as how to invent a machine or lay out a plant. And business men, engineers, and educators, can be just as ingenious and successful in doing it. It is the big field of industrial psychology, which for the twentieth century opens up like the nineteenth for chemistry and physics.

There is a narrow business or engineering psychology which overlooks this industrial psychology. It is the idea that the only interesting thing is the amount of compensation an individual can get, and so, by experimenting and measuring, we find out about how much bonus or premium is necessary in order to get him to do his best. This undoubtedly will work for a while, and will work for some individuals more than others, and for the young more than the old, but if it is too stimulating its effects are like intoxication. When the dream is over the awakening is sour.

Industrial psychology is more temperate. It looks ahead and measures the after effects. It sees not only a lot of isolated individuals, each hustling for himself, but sees the whole plant, the team work, the going concern, the joint product, the goodwill of employer and fellow-workers. And industrial psychology is willing to take some chances on the outcome.

Yes, it is said, a big and rich corporation can try experiments and take big chances; the little man must play safe. But look about, and see how little men become big. It is by plunging a little on a new idea. The new idea today is the interest and loyalty of workers. They are free and organizing as never before. Courts, legislatures and governments cannot be depended upon as in the past to coerce them. The business man with the new idea will get their interest and loyalty. Some will fail, others will succeed. But the chances of failure are probably greater by sticking to the old ideas than by venturing on the new ones.

For loyalty today is not the loyalty of former days. The slave was loyal because he could not quit. The laborer is loyal if he has no alternative to go elsewhere. He is loyal in hard times and disloyal in good times.

The new idea of loyalty is the loyalty of those to whom unemployment is no penalty. The law of hiring and firing has no coercion for them. They can find another job, or can wait until they find it. The new loyalty is the loyalty, not of penalties, but of goodwill. It is not afraid to quit or be fired, but willingly stays and works. And this kind of loyalty is not an inborn instinct of workmanship, but must be taught and drawn out by education, and kept up by continuous effort on the part of the employer. There is no asset so fragile as goodwill. The least inattention loses the customer. A year or two of careless attention destroys many years of previous effort.

In hard times, when workers are not free to quit, no attention need be paid to the cultivation of loyalty.

The coercive penalty is enough.   But it is at that very time that goodwill is won or lost.   The disloyalty of good times when workers are free to quit, has been produced by inattention to goodwill in the preceding hard times.   The employer who weeds out with a club in hard times and complains of disloyalty and lack of interest in good times, has not yet adapted himself to the new kind of loyalty that is built up, not on penalties, but on freedom.

Thus education, interesting work and loyalty go together.   Loyalty is not gratitude for past favors, nor a sense of obligation, but is expectation of reciprocity.   If the future is not to be better than the past, then gratitude loses its hold.   Education is not the teaching of gratitude or obligation for favors received, but is the unfolding of possibilities in the job and the worker.   It is this that makes work interesting and converts loyalty into goodwill.

XV

PERSONALITY

In the old romantic days the employer and his journeyman and apprentice lived and worked together, much as the small farmer does now with his hired help. But those were rather miserable days. There is nothing very romantic either for the hired man or the farmer, much less for the farmer's wife. It is not very regrettable that industry has gotten away from that personal touch. Long hours, compulsory association with each other out of working hours are not conducive to personality.

For personality is a kind of specialization. You need to get away. You need a little time for yourself. You need to be different. You need to specialize. The modern corporation has more chances for personality than ever were known before in industry. And it succeeds for that reason. If it has no monopoly it succeeds because it has a soul.

Goodwill is the soul; and goodwill is a multiple of all the different personalities that keep the business agoing. For personality is not mere individuality. It is that aspect of individuality that gets results. And specialization is not mere peculiarity. It is thorough preparation for the work of personality. Personality is power. It gets other people to do things. But it is not physical or economic power. You do not need much personality if you use a club or can keep the other man from getting a living. Personality is psychological power—the power of persuasion—the power to get across with free men. It is the child of liberty and democracy.

The modern corporation specializes in personality. And it specializes in the directions where those it deals with are free to go elsewhere. One kind of personality is successful in dealing with bankers, financiers, and investors. A somewhat similar in dealings with wholesalers and other manufacturers. A rather different kind is sent out on the road to reach the retailers. The auditors and accountants have their characteristic qualities. Lawyers and lobbyists are selected according to the personalities they meet in courts, politics and legislatures. The engineers, superintendents, and foremen are selected to get out product and buy the commodity labor.

More recently, as labor becomes more free or intractable, the labor psychologist is taken on. First, perhaps, the trade unionist who knows the mind of organized labor in the shop and in union meetings and headquarters. Then a variety of labor specialists— nurses, safety experts, health experts, welfare workers, scientific managers, educators, employment managers, service workers.

Naturally, these begin with the more obvious physical aspects of their work. The employer is inclined at first to be disappointed if his safety expert is not a mechanical engineer. He thinks of safety in terms of belts and set-screws.

But the safety expert does not produce safety, he sells it. The factory may be mechanically fool-proof. But that will hardly cut out more than one-third or one-half of the accidents. The workingmen must *buy* safety. It costs them something to play safe. They must keep their mind on it. They must look out. They must slow up. They must run the risk of irritating the foreman who is paid for output.

So, the safety expert must sell safety also to the foreman. It costs the foreman more than it does the workman. The foreman must be shown. He may not be able to see the pain and suffering. He has been brought up on accidents, and even thinks he has no accidents, when the truth is that he did not notice them. He must get a bigger idea. He must be led to see that, in the long run, safety increases the output of his men as a whole. It saves time and absence and turnover. The foreman must be educated to see himself as a going concern and not to see merely the irritating individual who plays safe.

To sell safety to the foreman it must be sold to the employer. It costs the employer more than it does the others. The smallest cost is what he spends in money on safe-guarding machines and plant. The largest cost is interference with production. He must let his safety expert have some authority over the foreman who thinks that safety reduces output. He must let him get the workmen together in committees.

Thus the safety engineer must be a social engineer. If he can invent and educate the "safety spirit" among the entire force from top to bottom, then the workmen and foremen will invent and demand and use more safety devices than he ever could think out and install by himself. He adds his personality to the going concern. He gives the corporation a soul.

And the nurse and doctor. The employer at first thinks of "first aid," or headaches, or fainting spells, or a medicine chest and cots and operating tables. He orders his nurse not to go out into the shop at all. The doctor is called only after the thing happens.

But the nurse and doctor must also sell health-first to the workers. They quit work, lay-off, or slow-up. The foreman loses their output and that is about all he has time to investigate. The nurse and doctor know more. The workers need to be encouraged to complain in advance of serious complaint. The employer needs to be shown the value of health. How far the nurse and doctor will be able to go, whether into the shop or even into the homes, is limited by their personality. One may offend and do harm. Another may be welcome. A mechanical expert in the hospital is one thing. People *must* come in extremity. A social expert who can carry the spirit of good health to the entire working force is something additional. The one may make the hospitals and beds look nice in photographs. The other gives a soul to the corporation.

And so on down the line of all the possible labor specialists. The great aim of them all is to make the work interesting and the workers willing. All are educators.

In the olden time the apprentice learned a trade by imitating the journeyman. When once learned the trade was fixed and irrevocable. But modern industry is revolutionary. It breaks up the trades just because it is based on underlying principles of chemistry, physics, psychology, which have thousands of different ways of working out in practice. The routine worker who only can imitate is left behind. The one who can contrive new ways of doing things that will work gets ahead.

We hear much of a "suggestion system." Workers are encouraged to write out their suggestions for improvements and send them in. Not many are real improvements, perhaps, but whether the system works or not depends on the personality that conducts it. If a worker offers a suggestion it is because his mind has waked up a little. If he is turned down without knowing why or if he hears nothing of it, he sinks back in a rut. If he gets a hearing or a voice in the decision, and learns why one suggestion is an improvement and another is not, then the system may accomplish the object, not mainly of getting a few improvements, but of getting the workers interested in the business.

The busy foreman or superintendent cannot spend much time on fruitless ideas. His job is output of product. What is wanted is output of ideas. It begins with the education of the beginner. When the boy or girl enters the shop he is full of questions, of untried ideas, of suggestions. If he is simply "broken in," so as to become productive as soon as possible, his questioning is suppressed. If he tries out his ideas he learns to select those that work and the reasons for rejecting the others. Then when he passes out from the "vestibule school" he is still a questioner. He comes back to that school to try out his ideas. The vestibule school becomes a graduate school. His education never is finished as long as he has a question or an untried idea.

A new labor department is thus created—the educational department. A new specialist is called for—the teacher. Not the hand-me-down teacher who passes on the traditions of the trade or shop, but the dig-it-up teacher who is an investigator along with every worker, old or young, who has a question or a suggestion. A new personality is called for, not the foreman who can get out product, but the teacher who can get out ideas.

The factory has its scientific laboratory for a select number of chemists or engineers, with their tests, experiments and installation of new devices. Every factory can have its educational department for all the workers who have questions and new ideas. But, if so, it all depends on the personality of the teacher.

A humdrum, routine teacher, who does it all himself, and demands imitation and repetition, is not a teacher. The one who can provoke ideas, raise doubts, stimulate ambitions, and then let the others do it themselves, he is the teacher. And he, too, may impart a soul to the corporation—the soul of hope, personality, individuality, self-reliance, in the workers because their work is interesting, promising and unfinished. He, too, may impart the loyalty that is goodwill —the loyalty that gladly sees their own progress in the progress and prosperity of the business. Here is the true science of scientific management.

It is the defect of every new idea that it gets standardized for the sake of those who do not understand it. Strong personalities have pioneered the movement for scientific management. They have understood human nature. They have come up through the shop and have been a part of the psychology of labor. They have known how to invent and sell efficiency to the worker. But when the movement spreads and large contracts are taken, smaller men are put into the shop with their instruments of measurement and their statistics and blue prints. Hoxie found that the mass of time-study men in the shops who actually set the tasks and make the piece and premium rates are "poorly paid and not men of an intellectual or moral quality and breadth of training and education" calculated to inspire confidence. There are exceptional individuals at the top, but for the staff that does the actual work the details are reduced to mechanical routine without a grasp of the social effects or labor problems that ensue.[1]

But the virtue of true scientific management is that it never is finished. It always has a fringe of trial and experiment. It always is ready to abandon a previous standard for something better. It is along this fringe of comparison and experiment that interest in one's work is to be found. If the worker does not share in this experimental side of his work, the interesting part of it is taken away from him and monopolized by the scientific manager. The great field of scientific management is to make the work interesting for the worker.

I know an inventor who was trying to work out in practice a new mechanical device. His laboratory experiments were perfect. His employer accepted them and gave him every facility for introducing them in the factory. The workers were indifferent and interested only in their wages. The factory experiments were disappointing. Finally he made the employees partners in the experiments. Immediately a multitude of practical suggestions began to

[1] Hoxie, R. F., *Scientific Management and Labor* (1915), pp. 113–122.

come from them and the device rapidly became practicable. He had tapped an unknown reservoir of ideas and experience that may be found in every factory.

I do not say that the factory should be converted into a laboratory for experiments. I only say that the labor department of the factory should have its experimental department, where new ideas are welcome and every worker with an idea can take part. But, of course, it depends on the personality that conducts the department. Here is the great field opening up for scientific management. The leaders and pioneers appreciate it.[1] Two things especially stand in its way: the demand of employers for quick results and the notion that workmen are interested only in the pay envelope.

The scientific manager may get quick results, may reduce costs and increase output and profit, but if he does it at the expense of losing the interest of the workers, then quick results bring increased costs elsewhere in the unrest and indifference of labor. And the pay envelope is of course important. It takes no genius to arouse interest in the pay envelope. But it takes some ingenuity and personality to arouse interest in the work that goes along with the pay. Very nice and accurate computations may be made of just the amount of payment by premiums, bonuses, or piece-rates, that is necessary to get the worker to exert himself. "Payment-by-results" keeps the money inducement uppermost at every hour of the

[1] See, for example, the experiments made by R. B. Wolf and reported in the *Bulletin of the Society to Promote the Science of Management*, August, 1915, March, 1917; *Proceedings of the Employment Managers' Conference, Philadelphia, Pennsylvania, April 2 and 3, 1917*, Bulletin 227, United States Bureau of Labor Statistics.

day, and crowds out other inducements. To get as much money as he can for as little effort or thought as he must give up, becomes the main idea of the piece worker and bonus worker. It requires no genius or personality to get this idea into the worker's head. Piece-work and bonus work are mechanical substitutes for personality. The factory is wound up, as it were, like a machine, with its wheels and cogs adjusted to a schedule of prices, and the operator can go away and let it work itself.

But personality cannot go away. It is the life of a going concern. It is always on the job. The schedule of prices is a schedule of thousands of labor contracts. The labor contract cannot be tied up like a mortgage. It is a new contract, a new agreement, every hour of the day and every day in the year. The up-to-date merchant does not employ even the cheapest clerk who merely throws down the goods with their labeled prices on the counter and lets the customer take it or leave it. So the up-to-date employer does not employ the foreman, straw boss, superintendent, manager, who only knows how to figure out prices and lets the worker take it or leave it.

For personality can be created. The merchant, whether he knows it or not, has his school of salesmanship, the employer his school of foremanship. Personality of a kind is taught, or perhaps only picked up, in the one and in the other. But not many employers have their school of personality with its separate organization for creating personality. It goes without saying that the candidate must know the mechanical details of figuring and getting out the work. But that is not personality. Likewise he must have a minimum of native character on which to build. But mere individuality is not personality.

Personality is individuality plus power—it is the psychology of influence without the power of compulsion. It is developed by trial and error; by experiment, success and failure; by exchange of ideas and experiences; by study of leadership; by self-examination; by cultivating health, vitality, courage, initiative, self-confidence, enthusiasm, and, above all, sympathy with the other man's point of view, imagination that puts one's self in his place, and sincerity that inspires his confidence.

People are not born with these qualities; they are not acquired by accident; the public schools may not have learned how to teach them; vocational schools may overlook them; but modern industry and democracy require them. And the business corporation can teach them when the proprietors see that they need them.

For the corporation can specialize in personality. This is the meaning of the movement to set up a "labor department," a "division of personnel," an "employment" or "service" department, a "trade board" or "board of arbitration," in the factory, on an equality with the sales department, the financial department, or the production department. The labor department is the school of personality that deals with labor. Throughout its entire personnel, from the nurse, doctor, the safety and welfare experts, the apprenticeship school, the vestibule school, to the foreman, the scientific manager, the employment manager, its standards of success are the interest, loyalty, goodwill, of labor. Each member of its staff is a mediator between capital and labor. To their technical knowledge of the needs of the business must be added the personality that wins the confidence of employer and employee.

But personality cannot be created by commands nor bought with money. The sham may *take* orders from above and be subject to the employer's will in all details. But the true is independent. It *issues* orders, even to the employer, and it cannot be bought because it has risen to the level of a profession whose members look for the approval of others in the profession over and above the approval of their employer. They do what is "right," not what they are ordered to do; they have sold to the employer, not themselves, but their professional advice of what he ought to do.

We see this new profession forming itself about us and beginning to fill the gap between capital and labor. Its literature is taking shape. Its conventions and conferences are held where experiences are exchanged, experiments compared, scientific principles developed; where professional ethics, professional enthusiasm and pride in a noble calling are lifting its members above dependence on any particular employer who happens to hire them. They are beginning to lay down the law, not of coercion, but the law of good-will—the law of health and safety, of vocational training, the law of employment, promotion, dismissal, payment of wages, and all the other relationships of capital and labor. They are beginning to be a new personality in industry.

The very separation of capital and labor and the concentration of absentee ownership calls them forth and opens the gap for them to occupy. It

11

cannot be expected that all capitalists or employers will recognize them as a profession or yield to them that independence in the shop without which they cannot develop. It requires considerable breadth of view to be willing to submit to constitutional government. The exercise of power in all its details seems in itself to be attractive even though it costs something at times. To come out on top is gratifying, even at the expense of goodwill and personality in others. For such employers there seems to be no remedy except the superior power of trade unions or government. I have seen a marked change occur in the character of an employer through the influence of a successful strike. Not that he becomes merely conciliatory and willing to compromise, but that his convictions and ethical beliefs themselves undergo a change. He listens, gets the point of view, regrets his oversight, is interested in remedying unnoticed abuses, patient in handling unfounded grievances. It is then that he welcomes the specialist, defers to another's judgment, enlarges his labor department, gives his mediators a free hand.

And the right kind of legislation and administration of labor laws has a similar effect. A certain employer, who regularly kicked out the factory inspector, ended by prosecuting him in court. But when the workmen's compensation law came in, with its automatic penalties for all accidents, he proudly sat with the inspectors and the representatives of labor, and helped them on behalf of the employers to frame up the safety rules to govern his business. In this way, unionism and government, properly conducted, are a factor in creating personality. They eliminate coercive power and call forth mental and moral power.

Personality has been and always will be the controlling figure in industry. Carnegie could pick out a Schwab or a Frick, place a tremendous inducement before him, then go away on long vacations and let the business run itself. Rockefeller could surround himself with geniuses. But personality in the past could succeed in the few because it was lacking in the many. It could use thousands and even millions of immigrants from the oppressed nationalities of Europe whose ignorance and submissiveness were the product of conquest.

The new America promises to be an educated America. "Americanization" means the spread of independence in the shop. The individuals cannot be swung in a mass by the boss, or the labor agent, or the padrone, but may be expected to assert themselves. Great and exceptional personalities there will be. But they will work through hundreds and thousands of lesser ones. The Carnegies and Rockefellers of the future will not only pick out a few but will train many of them, all along the line, for the thousands of positions where the interests and prejudices of labor must be consulted.

And the laborers themselves are producing their own leaders with their own ideas and personalities. The kind of leaders that they put forward is largely determined in the end by the kind that the capitalists select to meet them. At first they make mistakes. They elect fool committees to represent them. They have never been consulted and they suddenly acquire a feeling of power and self-importance. They must

learn by their own mistakes. Here is the hardest
test of personality on the part of the employer and
his representatives—the patience and ability to consult with those who have not yet learned how to
govern themselves.

In the end it is not masses or leaders, or committees,
that are dealt with. It is each individual worker in the
shop. Labor moves in a mass because that is the
way its individuals get more liberty and power.
What the individuals want determines what their
leaders demand.

It is in the daily and hourly dealings with every
worker in the shop that their ideas are formed and
their demands are formulated. There is where their
committees and leaders get their ideas and support.
There is where the employer's personality counts—
not a great personality at the top but scores and hundreds of personalities at every point and every hour
of contact with every worker in the shop. The employer who has learned how to select and train these
subordinates, who has his school of personality for
those who represent him in his dealings with labor,
is the one who is beginning to meet the situation.

A certain amount of idealism and imagination is
needed to grasp these new conditions and possibilities.
Says the "director of personnel" in a great corporation, "a new heaven and a new earth are being made
in the thinking along this line." But, he goes on,
"the promotion of such a view point might be difficult with the usual general manager unless the
employment manager had a better standing than he
ordinarily has." In his particular establishment the
"division of personnel" has this recognized standing

as a part of the whole enterprise, and for this reason he hopes to work out "something worth while."

It goes back to the board of directors, the stock-holders, even the bankers and creditors. If they are not converted to this new heaven and new earth, then there is no place for a "director of personnel." He is a dreamer, a utopist, to be tied down by strict orders from above. He is suspected of ignorance of human nature. He is raising dangerous hopes of collective bargaining. His mistakes weigh heavy and he is given no chance to make mistakes. He is reduced to the level of a routine worker. But with a little imagination on the part of capitalists that can picture the daily life of the workers in their shops, with a little idealism that can picture something different from what they are accustomed to, the personnel department may rise to a recognized place as industry's school of personality.

And the reason why this personnel department is attaining this high recognition is because the labor problem has ceased to be a problem merely of the demand and supply of labor. The personnel depart-ment is not the employment department. It is not the department of hiring and firing. It is the department that deals with every human relation within and without the establishment. It is the depart-ment of industrial goodwill. It is the department of justice as well as the department of health and efficiency. It is the department of personality. Raised to its proper place of equality with other departments it is the department that guides the entire establishment in the administration of justice, industrial welfare, and service to the nation

With such an exalted position its motto for its own guidance may well become that same "due process of law" which guides the judicial branch of government under the American Constitution. No citizen may be deprived of life, liberty, or property without due process of law. But he may be deprived *with* due process of law. No worker may be deprived of his job, which is labor's life, liberty and property, without due process of law. Due process signifies investigation of all the facts in the case and due weight given to each fact before decision is made. Investigation signifies the right to a hearing in order that all the facts may be known. Due weight signifies that the conflicting facts in the case shall be weighed, and each shall be given its just weight and importance in making up the final decision.

No single case is like any other, and no establishment is like any other establishment. The facts are always different and must therefore be weighed. But they are always weighed according to the theory and purpose entertained by him who weighs them. If the judge or employment manager looks upon labor as a commodity, then he weighs the facts according to the theory of demand and supply. If he looks upon labor as a machine he gives weight to the facts that get maximum output from the individual. If he entertains the goodwill theory then the facts that promote goodwill are looked for and get a proper emphasis in his mind. If he sees in labor the great foundation of national welfare and national integrity then the facts that promote patriotism get due weight in his mind. If he finds a place in his heart for the notions of solidarity, partnership, and democracy of capital and labor, then the facts that lead in that direction get larger emphasis and are seriously investigated and found.

Only the foolish, the ignorant, the biased or the arbitrary man ties himself up to a single theory. Every theory has its proper place as an instrument in weighing the facts. It is this that is due process of law. This is investigation of all the facts and due weight given to each.

And it is this that gives to personality its highest attribute—"reasonableness." The employment manager, the scientific manager, the welfare worker, the foreman, the superintendent, any or all of the employer's representatives, may have all of the technical qualities needed, but if he does not have reasonableness he fails. And reasonableness can be cultivated in the personnel department, like any other quality. It is just ordinary common sense raised to the level of a science. It is more than scientific management, it is scientific justice. It is more than personnel, it is personality. It is ability, not only to see all the facts but to hunt for them and find them. It is capacity to give every man a hearing; capacity to distinguish the true and the false; capacity to distinguish the essential and the non-essential; capacity to inspire confidence by reason of sincerity and open-mindedness; above all, it is capacity to be guided by that grand purpose of promoting public welfare that should guide all industry and that gives to industry a noble place in the nation's life.

XVI

DEPRESSION

A curve showing the movement of prices during the nineteenth century is a picture of cycles of prosperity and depression.[1] Wholesale prices are employer's prices. While wholesale prices are moving upward, profits are increasing.

Retail prices are the cost of living. Retail prices lag five or six months behind wholesale prices and do not rise as high or fall as low as wholesale prices.[2]

The rise in employer's prices and profits increases the demand for labor. The unemployed are set to work, and those already employed get more work. Without an increase in wages, the *earnings* of labor on the whole are increased. Finally, the wages begin to rise with the rise in retail prices, or cost of living, and consequently earnings increase under the two-fold influence of higher rates of wages and more work.

The downward movement is the reverse. Retail prices and wages lag several months behind the fall in wholesale prices. Profits decline, laborers are laid off or put on short time, and, while the rates of wages remain relatively high, unemployment or slack employment reduces the earnings of labor.

For a hundred years this wave has been moving up and down across all the nations that have been bound

[1] Figure I.
[2] Figure II.

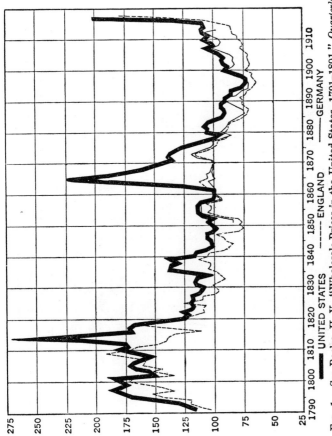

Fig. 1.—See Roelse, H. V., "Wholesale Prices in the United States, 1791–1801," *Quarterly Publications of the American Statistical Association*, December 1917, pp. 840–846; Commons and Associates, *History of Labor in the United States*, Vol. I. p. 11.

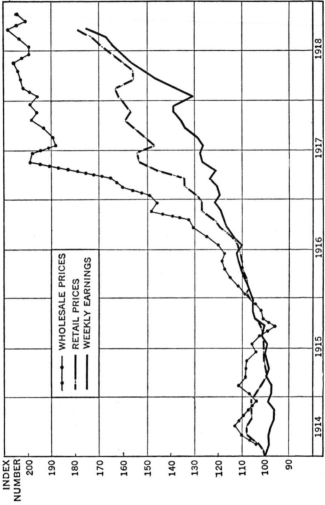

Fig. 2.—For wholesale prices, see *The Annalist*, New York. For retail prices, see U. S. Department of Labor, *Monthly Review*. For weekly earnings, see New York Industrial Commission, Monthly Labor Market Report.

together by transportation and commerce. The curve of prices and wages for America is substantially the curve for Europe. And in all countries it has had its reflection in labor movements and politics. During the rise in prices and profits labor becomes aggressive. Labor unions are organized, short and successful strikes multiply, wages are advanced without strikes. During the fall in prices labor unions are less aggressive, strikes on a falling market are less successful, and laborers turn to politics, protective tariffs, socialism, panaceas or even revolution. The long depression from 1837 to 1848 was the period of Chartism in England; socialism, anarchism, revolution in Europe; protective tariff and humanitarian reforms in America. The prosperity that began in 1850 was the beginning of modern trade unionism in England and America and the restoration of monarchy in Europe. The Civil War period was one of prosperity and labor organization in America and Europe, followed by the long depression, until 1879, with its greenbackism, anarchism, socialism, and the decline of trade unionism. The recovery after 1880 and the ups and downs since that time are reflected in the enlargement of trade unionism when labor has been in demand, and political and socialistic panaceas when unemployed.[1]

The wave climbed another summit in the midst of the great war—an artificial height raised up by the demands of governments and the substitution of credit for money. Yet, unlike former periods, prices, profits, wages and strikes were controlled and supplies

[1] Figure III. See also Commons and Associates, *History of Labor in the United States.*

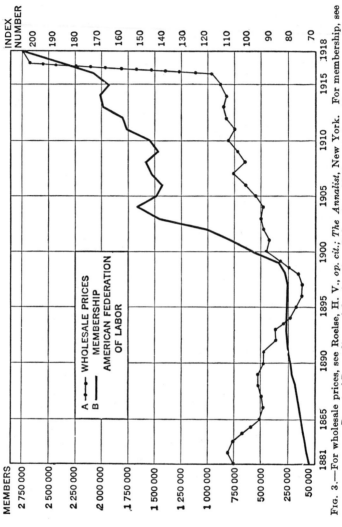

FIG. 3.—For wholesale prices, see Roelse, H. V., *op. cit.*; *The Annalist*, New York. For membership, see *Report of Proceedings of the American Federation of Labor*, 1918, p. 44.

were rationed by the governments. Even a League of Nations was created with not only its army but also its international board of food controllers and its centralized boards of control over the world's industries, finance and shipping.

With the break-up of this national and international control, the world again faces a period of depression while competitive prices and wages are again seeking their lower levels. Notwithstanding the destruction of war, labor reached a high level of wages and earnings in terms of money, on both sides of the battle line, unknown in time of peace. With these high prices and wages employers cannot be expected to shift from war to peace while they are uncertain as to the future decline of prices and wages.

The World War silenced for a time the contest of capital and labor. Employers submitted to regulations designed to eliminate profits by means of cost contracts and excess taxes. Organized labor yielded the right to strike in view of governmental regulation of wages, hours and conditions of employment. Patriotism united capital and labor. But with the return of peace and depression, this tie of patriotism is loosened.

At the same time, organized labor in all lands reached a political influence unknown hitherto. Its leaders were admitted to a share along with capitalists in the governmental control of industry. While they yielded the right to strike, they gained a voice in the regulation of prices, profits and wages. No previous war or previous prosperity offers a parallel.

Yet, just as in previous periods, outside the ranks of organized labor, certain interests that are quiescent in time of prosperity come forth when aggressive labor is weakened by depression and unemployment. At the one extreme are those business interests which since the Civil War have controlled American industry, again looking forward to a return of their uncontrolled liberty in home affairs but also looking forward to a new power and a new assistance of government in enlarging foreign markets and foreign investments. For them, the period of depression serves to weaken the power of organized labor in industry and government and to strengthen their own promises to labor of a return of prosperity, if they have control.

At the other extreme are the class known in Europe as the "intellectuals"—physicians, lawyers, professors, politicians, economists—the leaders in socialism, anarchism, politics, and other promises to labor, who, in times of depression and unemployment compete successfully with the leaders of organized labor for the support of labor.

Each period of depression and unemployment for a hundred years has seen this rivalry of capitalistic politicians and labor politicians for the support of labor. In Europe it has been the contest over socialism, anarchism, syndicalism, culminating in the revolutions of 1848 and the reaction of 1850; or the revolutions of 1917 and 1918. In America it has been contests over protective tariffs, greenbackism, silver, monopolies, and control of the courts. The labor politicians offer to labor political power over capital; the capitalistic politicians offer employment and wages.

Hitherto, in no period of depression, either in Europe or America, have organized workers and or-

ganized employers joined together on a large scale
to eliminate the intellectuals and the politicians and
to tide over the depression by their own self-governing
arrangements. Perhaps it is too much to expect,
notwithstanding the evident advantages that might
be gained. While the control remains merely a contest for power, each takes advantage of all the agencies
that augment its power at the expense of the other.
In times of prosperity organized labor gets the upper
hand; in times of depression, organized employers.
But the Great War revealed another motive, patriotism, that mitigates the struggle for power.

While the "intellectuals" or labor politicians might
have taken advantage of the situation to make labor
the supreme power, the leaders of organized labor
restrained their followers. For, supreme power in
the hands of labor means, not the supremacy of
labor, but supremacy of the labor politician. In
Russia it has not been the workingmen who rose to
power, but the "intellectuals" who made impossible
promises to labor. The "dictatorship of the proletariat" became the dictatorship of labor politicians.

The leaders of organized labor, especially in England and America, have a different training. They
have come up through the shop. They are "manu-
als," not "intellectuals." They have known what
it is to lose out when they strike for the impossible.
They are aggressive but practical. They realize,
for the most part, that laborers cannot govern the
nation if they cannot govern themselves. More
important to them than illusory or extravagant
gains in wages that may soon be lost, is the preservation of their union which preserves what they gain.

Like all good business men they demand more than they expect to get. Their position is difficult. They are between the demands of employers, the promises of the intellectuals and politicians on the outside, and their critics and rivals on the inside.

The outcome often depends on the attitude of the employers, or rather of the representatives and leaders whom the employers put forward as their spokesmen. For they too speak through their leaders. If they select leaders to represent them, lawyers, intellectuals, and experts, whose only idea is power and the inalienable rights of the employer, then organized labor is likely to discredit its own cautious leaders and put forth others whose only argument is power and the inalienable rights of labor.

I knew a great labor organization whose leaders were able during a period of depression to get their rank and file to accept successive reductions of wages. But it was because the employers granted that indispensable condition, the preservation of the union. With the union preserved against discrimination and victimization of its leaders and officers, it could, in coöperation with the employers, distribute the hardships of unemployment and reduced earnings among all its members.

The situation here, as in all other industrial relations, goes back to the question of personality, and that final test of personality, reasonableness. Industry creates personality by education and selection. The outsider, the intellectual, the politician, can never attain the level of reasonableness because he never can know by experience all of the facts that must be given due weight in reaching a plan of action.

When employers and employees understand each other and are striving not only for power but for reasonable solutions under the circumstances, they do not need the outsider, however much they may rely upon him in other matters. Only when they rest their final appeal on force and power and inalienable rights, does the outsider seem to have a place, and then his greatest service to both is the elimination of himself as soon as possible.

For the proper place of the "intellectual" or expert, so-called, is that of the *agent* and not that of the *principal*. The principals in industry are the associated employers and the associated employees. The expert's place is that of attorney, statistician, accountant, economist, mediator, adviser, agent, in short, employee— of the principals. The principals determine what shall be done, their agents execute it. The agent becomes the expert because he is a specialist, and that signifies that he knows only the details of a small part of all the facts that must be weighed in reaching a decision. If the principals abdicate, and government by experts takes their place, the result is no less arbitrary and coercive than other forms of autocracy. It may be "scientific," so-called, but it conceals in the name of science its ignorance of facts belonging to a different science.

For no one person and no class of persons, however expert, can truly represent in due proportion all of the interests that clash and must be reconciled in reaching a final decision. Only the interests themselves, that is, the principals, must decide.

For this reason the great captains of industry themselves must come forward and deal with organized

12

labor directly instead of leaving it to their agents. The captains are the stockholders, bondholders, investors, bankers, financiers. Modern capitalism hides, as it were, in the background, and puts forward its lawyers, its presidents of corporations, its general managers, its lobbyists, its agents.

However expert and even fair-minded these agents are, they have no discretion outside their limited field, and they cannot take into account all of the facts, both because they do not truly know them and because they have no authority to act on all the facts. They must win out at once, in the narrow field assigned to them. They cannot take into account all the facts in different fields. They cannot take fully into account patriotism, national welfare, the approaching national and international solidarity of labor, the remote future effects and reactions that are likely to follow, because they have no authority to do so. They may succeed in making capitalism powerful at a time when labor is weak, but they may undermine its foundations when labor is strong or goes into politics. Only the principals themselves can take into account all of these other considerations, and they cannot weigh them if their only source of information is their own agents and experts. When Carnegie went on a long vacation the Homestead strike occurred. Today a similar strike might possibly spread to the nation or world. Thirty years ago, an individual capitalist might act by himself. Today the associated capitalists of the nation and even of the world cannot avoid either personal or joint responsibility.

Neither can organized labor act through advocates,

retainers, lawyers, intellectuals, politicians. These may, for the moment, win a glorious victory, but they leave a sting. They do not personally suffer the after effects, because they do not go back into the shop to earn their living. Immediate and stunning results are enough for them. The long look ahead, the future daily bargainings and negotiations in the shop, the preservation of the union in time of depression, the give-and-take that maintains goodwill, cannot weigh very heavily on them in the flush and thrill of putting the employer in a hole and getting the applause of labor.

On the continent of Europe the leaders of organized labor are often from the professional classes. To them, a remote future of socialism or syndicalism, when labor shall be supreme, is more impressive than getting along with the foremen or managers in the shop tomorrow and next day. Such leaders can advance themselves in politics or professional practice, and do it even more successfuly on account of the unsettled grievances or the troubles that they can stir up, in the shop. Their leadership is proof either of the immaturity and ignorance of the workers or of the failure of employers to deal directly with their employees.

Much the same is true of labor leaders themselves who have dropped the idea of returning to the shop to earn their living and are looking forward to a life of politics or insurance agency or professional practice. They have ceased truly to represent labor, for it is not a person's memory of the past that guides his acts but his expectations of the future. Neither the employer who has come up from the shop nor the

labor leader who does not expect to go back to the
shop can give due weight to the expectations of the
workers in the shop.

For this reason the labor leader who, as in England,
attempts to combine the two activities of member of
Parliament and leader of his union, eventually finds
that new leaders, directly out of the shop, are put
forward to assert the claims of the rank and file.
This is one of the reasons for the "shop steward"
movement previously mentioned,[1] for the shop stewards are but committees of shop workers. They are
the real principals for they are the workers themselves
who expect to return to work.

"In England, members of Parliament formerly
were not paid salaries from the public treasury and
the labor leaders in Parliament received their salaries
from their unions. This has been changed and they
no longer depend on their unions for their salaries.
In America, where the political salaries are paid by
the tax payers, the attempt to combine the position
of politician and labor leader in one man is not
practicable. When elected, the leader becomes independent of the workers and looks to other classes
for support in the elections."

For this and similar reasons the progress of democracy is forcing the separation of government into two
branches, the industrial and the political.

This separation has been dimly recognized by the
socialists of Germany. In that country, socialism,
their political branch of the labor movement, arose
before unionism, the industrial branch. The two
have been kept separately organized, though the

[1] Above, p. 118.

separation has been largely on paper, because the same individuals have retained leadership in each.

In Russia they have not been kept separate and consequently when Russia was on the verge of adopting a political government that should represent all classes, the combination of manual unionism and intellectual socialism set aside the constitutional convention called for that purpose, and proceeded to operate both industry and government by means of their sovyets, or associations of workingmen leaders and non-workingmen "intellectuals."

France, too, has not kept separate the political and industrial branches, and the Confederation of Labor has been both a political party and a national federation of labor unions.[1]

In England, both Parliament and trade unions had been long in existence in their separate fields and when the unions felt compelled, on account of hostile court decisions, to go into politics, they elected a number of their trade union leaders to Parliament (1906) and these, with the political socialists and later with the coöperative societies (1917), constituted themselves the British Labor Party. It is this mixing of the political and industrial activities that has begun to force recognition of their incompatibility through the shop steward movement just mentioned, and this has received recognition in the notable proposals by parliamentary committees and the Ministry of Reconstruction. Shop committees which, without recognition, had asserted themselves as a menace to British industry, are to be recognized and given a definite

[1] Estey, J. A., *Revolutionary Syndicalism*, p. 44.

standing in industry but not in politics.[1] Over and above these shop committees are the Industrial Councils for districts and the nation, to be encouraged and established in every industry where the representatives of employers and the industrial, but not political, representatives of the workers shall deliberate, shall agree on the larger policies and the minimum standards which then shall be recommended for adoption in the shops.

Where there are strong employers' associations and strong labor unions, extending over the shops of the kingdom, these recommendations are enforced without appealing to Parliament for compulsory powers. But where these organizations do not exist, then the so-called minimum wage boards, already existing in the sweat shop industries, are to be extended, with their compulsory powers of fixing wages, hours and conditions of labor.[2] Presumably these compulsory powers once applied will be withdrawn, or fall in abeyance, if the voluntary organizations arise with sufficient influence to take their place.

Without stopping to consider further details or the extent to which this program of reconstruction is practicable in all industries, the main purpose is evident. It is the creation, outside the parliamentary and political government of Britain, of representative industrial governments, as free as possible from the interference of those whose main interests are intellectual, professional, or political. If the plans succeed then

[1] Above, p. 119.

[2] *Monthly Review*, United States Bureau of Labor Statistics, May, 1918, pp. 59–61; September, 1918, pp. 53–58. Commons and Andrews, *Principles of Labor Legislation*, pp. 167–196.

England will have opened up two fields for the two different kinds of leaders and the two different kinds of problems to be met.

In the United States the two great political parties are organized and controlled like private corporations, and important legislation is determined not so much by members of Congress and the legislatures as by the party organizations which control those members. In matters of labor legislation, Congress is more a forum where the members issue campaign speeches to their constituents than the real law-making body. On this account the legislative efforts of both capitalists and organized labor are directed more toward influencing the party machine than toward electing their leaders to Congress or the legislatures. This secret influence of the lobbyists on both sides makes it even more urgent in America than in other countries, that industrial government should be separated from the political government, and that, if legislation is necessary it should first be agreed upon by organized employers and employees and then presented to the legislatures for adoption without material change through political influence.

The mine inspection and safety laws of the state of Illinois were for many years the plaything of politics, were unenforceable and loaded with "jokers." Finally, when the coal operators' association and the mine workers' union agreed on a code of safety, it was presented to the legislature and enacted into an enforceable and reasonable law. The workmen's compensation and accident prevention laws of various states have sometimes been drafted in this extra-political manner. Under the Industrial Commission laws of New York, Ohio and Wisconsin, this method of industrial legislation is applied to all branches of labor legislation.[1]

The temptation, of course, to break over and to use political influence on behalf of either class is great, but the most effective and workable legislation is probably that in which the two sides in good faith stand by their industrial government. The political government then remains, as it should, the instrument that protects the general interests of the public, furnishes the statisticians and similar experts, the mediators when employers and employees disagree, and the club that raises backward employers to the level of progressive ones.

This arrangement, of course, is impossible where either side refuses to deal with the other, or where one attempts to break down the organization of the other or to violate good faith by resorting to its political influence. It is then that the party politician, the intellectual, the lawyer, the lobbyist, breaks into and widens the gap between employer and employee. In times of prosperity and patriotism this is less likely. In times of depression and class struggle it is more likely.

Neither is the arrangement widely practicable as long as the main fight of organized labor is for the right to exist. The decisions of the Supreme Court in the Hitchman and other cases already referred to, continue to lie across the road to this reasonable

---

[1] See Commons, *Labor and Administration,* pp. 401–404; Commons and Andrews, *Principles of Labor Legislation,* pp. 430–443; *Final Report of the Commission on Industrial Relations* (1915), pp. 359–361.

goal. Not until they are reversed can labor unions keep out of politics.

It is not worth while to talk of ideal solutions. The problem is one, not of ideals but of alternatives. Ideals are usually the ideals of an individual or a class. The socialistic ideal ends, as we have seen, in the dictatorship of organized labor and the supremacy of intellectuals. The capitalistic ideal ends in conquest and imperialism. The problems of depression, of unemployment, of wages, hours of labor, conditions of work, efficiency, competition, are problems of adjustment and accommodation which must be met every day. It is not a "program" or a "platform" or a schedule of "inalienable rights" that bridges over the periods of hardship and depression, but it is the spirit of true democracy, which investigates, takes into account all of the facts, gives due weight to each, and works out, not an ideal, but a reasonable solution day by day.

The foregoing refers mainly to the legislative branch of government. We have already noted the conditions that apply to the administrative branch. It is here, far more than in legislation, that the daily coöperation of capital and labor is worked out. The Great War forced the nation to organize its administrative machinery on this basis, in order to increase the supply of munitions of war. The problems of peace and depression call for similar organization. The Federal Employment Service, operated nominally by government but actually by its advisory boards of employers and employees, should be the agency kept permanently in existence for dealing with depression and unemployment as it had begun

to deal with prosperity and employment.   The Labor
Policies Board, which during the war attempted to
bring together all of the agencies of government,
should become the really governing committee of
employer and employee authorized by and in aid of the
Department of Labor.   The War Labor Board with
its adjustment of disputes and its regulation of wages,
hours and methods of payment, should become
the National Joint Conference of Capital and Labor.

In each of these agencies the circumstances of war
made it necessary to have somewhat compulsory
powers.   Such powers are not needed in time of peace
except in minor particulars.   The industrial government of the nation must become mainly a voluntary
government, for its success in the long run will depend
not on power, but goodwill.

XVII

THE WORLD

Seventy years ago Karl Marx and his fellow socialists issued from London their Communist Manifesto.
Two great conclusions were proclaimed, pacifism and
internationalism. Both of these doctrines grew out of
what Marx interpreted to be the economic development of history. Modern industry had grown up
since the invention of the steam engine. Capitalism
had spread beyond the bounds of a single nation.
Capitalists knew no country and sought investments
and markets in all parts of the world where profits
could be obtained.

On the other hand, labor had nothing to expect from
the governments or capitalists of Europe. The workingmen of all nations must organize throughout all
nations. Because capital had become international,
labor organizations must become international.

And so, while Marx attacked both property and
government, he also held up to the workingmen a
grand ideal of the international brotherhood of labor.
Labor would ultimately, without any effort on its own
part but by the natural evolution of industry, come
into possession of the machinery of production. The
capitalists would disappear, and with them would
disappear nations.[1]

But there were certain forces which Karl Marx
underestimated. He underestimated the power of
patriotism. He might indeed disregard patriotism in

---

[1] *Communist Manifesto*, Chas. Kerr and Company, Chicago.

1848, for at that time the countries of Europe were split into small principalities, republics, and kingdoms. Italy had not yet attained unity. The German Empire was fifteen years ahead. Austria and Hungary were exploiting subject races. No one could very well picture a spirit of patriotism toward these principalities and oppressors.

But with the struggle in Italy which brought about Italian unity, with the struggles in Germany which founded the German Empire, more powerful than class struggle or the international brotherhood of man is the spirit of patriotism which binds together the peoples of a nation regardless of classes, and thus builds up what we have seen in our own nation since 1865—the spirit of nationality.

We have seen the socialists of a nation which, more than any other, had adopted socialism, the most powerful socialistic body in the world, the most orthodox in the Marxian doctrine, abandon their principles of internationalism and join with the capitalists of their own country to exploit the workingmen of the rest of the world. We have seen this spirit of patriotism degraded beneath the high principles of international brotherhood which Karl Marx had set before the workingmen of the world. Patriotism, a noble principle, recognized in all nations as something that should bring forward a better future for the world, became the very foundation of a cruel struggle for world empire and a denial of the brotherhood of labor.

Another thing that Karl Marx underestimated was trade unionism. In 1848 the world had just passed through, or was closing up, a period of depression in business. After the panic of 1837 the workingman's condition throughout Europe and America had been growing steadily worse. It was a long period of depression, of unemployment, of poverty and misery. On the basis of that experience of ten years, Karl Marx laid down the universal law that the progress of capitalism meant the pauperization of labor. So far as he had the facts up to date he was correct. Throughout the entire world, in Europe and in America, had grown up many varieties of anarchistic and socialistic doctrines. From that narrow foundation of history Karl Marx predicted a future in which the workingman would grow continually worse in his poverty, until ultimately his condition would become so bad, and capitalism itself would so completely have destroyed its own power, that the workingman would by some magic come into possession of those things which capitalism had created.

But what has happened since that time? It is only since 1850 that modern trade unionism has acquired any particular power. Modern labor organization began in England in the decade of the fifties and in America in the same decade, spreading afterward to Germany, France, and the world. This movement of trade unionism has been, not a passive submission of labor to economic evolution, but a struggle of labor to better its condition day by day. Karl Marx could not predict what trade unionism would accomplish. He could not see that labor, through its own organization, might ultimately be in a position to improve the conditions of labor, to raise wages, to shorten working hours.[1]

[1] See Commons and Associates, *History of Labor in the United States*, New York, 1918.

Neither does trade unionism offer an ideal solution
for the remote future.   It has no "program," which
means revolution.   It has only the every-day problem
of bettering the condition of labor under the existing
capitalistic government.   If that government is impe-
rialistic then trade unionism shares the fruits of imperialism.   In Germany we have seen the triumph of
trade unionism rather than the triumph of socialism.
We have seen labor unite with the capitalists to reduce
the workingmen and farmers of Russia to the status
of vassals for the sake of higher wages for German
labor and higher profits for German capital.

Another thing which Karl Marx overlooked was the
possibility of labor legislation.   When the Communist
Manifesto was written in 1848 there was but one
nation which had enacted any protective legislation on
behalf of the working people.   Only one year before
the Manifesto was written, England, after many years
of agitation, put on her statute books the first law in
the history of the world requiring that the labor of
women in industries be reduced to ten hours a day.
This first example of labor legislation had occurred
so shortly before the date of the Communist Manifesto
that its consequences could not be estimated.   But
since that time in all modern countries a great social
movement has brought about labor legislation in all
forms; the protection of women and children, minimum wages, industrial education.   All of these agencies have come forward to improve the condition of
labor, and it was Germany again which profited most
and first by this modern movement for such legislation.

Germany, under Prince Bismarck, who had brought
about German unity, now turned upon the socialists

in order to drive them out of Germany. In 1878 was enacted the famous anti-socialist law which prohibited all organizations of labor and all agitation and propaganda of socialistic doctrine. That law stood on the statute books of Germany until 1890—twelve years.

But it was not anti-labor legislation, it was pro-labor legislation that saved Germany. Immediately after the enactment of the anti-socialist law, Bismarck proceeded to introduce in Germany the measures for workmen's compensation, sickness insurance, health and invalidity insurance, old-age pensions—that notable series of indemnities for labor against the insecurity of accident, sickness, and misfortune.

Bismarck's policy was designed to undermine the influence of socialism, to win the workingmen away from the socialist movement and attach them to the government.

Following this came that other forward step in Germany, industrial and vocational education, in pursuance of which German employers consented that their workmen under the age of eighteen should be allowed as much as one day a week, on pay, to devote to an education in the trade or occupation in which they were engaged.

Thus Germany cemented the labor element to the Empire, and when, in 1914, the German government called upon the socialist leaders to go out with their propaganda into other nations and to break down the morale of Italy, France, and Russia, the argument which these leaders put forward to justify themselves was the claim that social legislation in Germany had done more for German workingmen than had been done by any other nation for its workingmen. England and

France entered upon this class of legislation long after Germany.   Other nations have been twenty or twenty-five years behind Germany in perceiving the national importance of social and labor legislation.

We in the United States have been more backward in this respect than any other great industrial nation, partly because we have had an unlimited supply of immigrants from European countries.   Our employers have not felt the need of conservation of labor because labor was plentiful.   The laborers who needed to be conserved were very few, because they already were more prosperous than in Germany or England.   And so employers have gone on in a contented way, believing that the labor supply of the nation was unlimited.   Relying upon our great natural resources and our inventive genius they have thought that we could stand up as a nation without necessarily protecting our laboring people.

But now we and all the nations perceive, as never before, that the next stage in industrial progress is not that economic revolution which Karl Marx predicted, it is not even development in machinery and tools, but it is the increased production and increased wealth of the world which are now dependent upon the health, intelligence, goodwill of labor. That nation which is foremost in giving heed to the health and housing, the vocational education, security and wages of its working people will be the nation which will survive even in times of peace. How much greater the need in war time of a strong, healthy, and intelligent working people!

Another thing that Karl Marx overlooked was the political power of capitalism.   According to all that

he could see at that time, the progress of industry
consisted in the big capitalists driving the small
capitalists out of business and absorbing the business.
In the final outcome it would naturally follow that a
few big capitalists would own all the industries, and
then it would be a very easy matter for the expropriated wage-earners simply to take possession.

But he did not know the possibilities of the modern
corporation. There were at that time very few
corporations in existence. The modern corporation
has diffused capitalism throughout large masses of
people by building up a system of stocks and bonds, of
savings banks and insurance companies, and millions
of people who, under the old Marxian theory, would
have been expropriated, have become themselves
members of the propertied and capitalist class.

The political power of capitalism was demonstrated
in Germany more fully than anywhere else in the
world. For no other nation had gone to the limit
reached by Germany in subsidizing its exporters and
importers, in subsidizing banks that had their ramifi-
cations throughout the world, in subsidizing syndicates
of all kinds which enabled the German capitalist to
spread his markets throughout the world, in purchasing railroads, building canals, and giving manufacturers differential advantages in order that they
might drive competitors from other markets. The
German government allied itself with capitalists,
and made a science of "dumping"—dumping their
products by underselling manufacturers of other
countries, and recouping the losses from taxes on the
German people. Having destroyed competitors in
foreign countries, they could perhaps get control of

13

those markets, and establish German monopoly. This tremendous power of modern business, which showed its largest fruit in the capitalistic socialism of the German Empire, is something that Karl Marx did not foresee.

These are the grand national and social forces which have come into existence since the time of the Communist Manifesto, and have nullified what otherwise might have been accurate predictions of that Manifesto. For Karl Marx had based his calculations upon the purely mechanical, economic evolution of machinery, of tools, of markets, of supply and demand. He had not weighed these spiritual and psychological forces which have revolutionized the modern world. He had not seen beneath the economic forces. He had not seen the power of patriotism by virtue of which the divers classes of these different nations would finally unite. He had not seen the movement of trade unionism through which laborers learned to organize, learned self-control, learned to negotiate with employers, learned that they need not fall back into the pauper condition that Marx predicted, but that by negotiation, by arbitration, they might make an agreement with the capitalists, that they might come to terms with the capitalists and divide the product between them.

The spirit of trade unionism, instead of being that of class struggle, is the spirit of partnership. The trade union movement looks upon itself, not as the irreconcilable opponent of capitalism, but as a member of the family. Being a member of the family it is entitled to have a row with the head of the family, and to live apart for a time, but it has not yet taken out a

divorce. Trade unionists do not presume, as Karl
Marx did, that the members of the family can do
without the head of the family. Trade unionism is
based upon that principle of partnership which we see
in a different way in the home. Consequently here
we have a spiritual movement which has not attacked
family, religion, and property, as Karl Marx had done,
but has organized itself to get a larger share of profits
by negotiation, by agreement, by strikes.

In America, when the war came on, the socialists
and their anarchistic partners, the Industrial Workers
of the World, promptly took the side of Karl Marx
with his theory of internationalism and were willing to
let Germany win. The trade unions just as promptly
took the side of America. Both had similar grievances
and similar aims. Both wanted more wages and
shorter hours of labor and better conditions of labor.
Both were organized to fight the capitalists.

But there was a world of difference. Nearly 3,000-
000 wage-earners were organized in trade unions.
Their employers recognized them and dealt with
their representatives. They had already established
representative democracy. These 3,000,000 wage-
earners already knew that they were a part of the
great American democracy. They knew that they
had an equal voice and equal power with capitalism.

The socialists, the Industrial Workers of the World,
the American Bolsheviki, hated American capitalism
and were willing to see it crushed by German capitalism. To them all capitalism was but industrial
autocracy and they saw no difference between American
and German autocracy. They held that capitalism
the world over must be destroyed and labor must

become the autocrat. They would have poisoned our minds with hatred and would have broken down our spirit as they did in Russia and nearly did in Italy.

But the trade union movement saved us. The trade unionists had their grievances against capitalists. They had gone through many bitter fights and were preparing for more. Not all capitalists would recognize them or meet their committees. In fact, only a minority of the employers of the country had dealings with organized laborers. But it was that minority that saved us. If they had been like the majority of employers then there would have been no organized labor ready to resist and overcome the socialists, the I.W.W. and the other Bolsheviks in our midst. Trade unionism justified itself and, next to our armies going to France, the greatest asset of America has been our trade union movement, and the greatest protection of American capitalism has been the capitalists who dealt with trade unions.

Karl Marx also overlooked that other spiritual force, that humanitarian spirit which might look upon the hardships of labor as something that should be immediately cured; that spirit which has led to the marvellous development of social legislation in which many employers have taken the lead. It has been the example of progressive employers for a hundred years that has shown what could be done. Then the influence of politics has come forward to make universal among employers that which progressive capitalists had done voluntarily in their own factories. This humanitarianism of capital, this spiritual force which can look forward, in a humanitarian as well as in a business way, to the improved condition of the working population, this spiritual and social principle, he did not recognize.

And now we in this country, as in all other countries, are in a position to learn the lesson of history of the past seventy years. We can free ourselves entirely from the idea that economic forces, that supply and demand alone, are to determine the destiny of this nation or any other nation. That destiny will be determined by the spiritual forces, the forces of solidarity, the forces of coöperation, the forces of partnership on the one hand and struggle on the other. It is that nation which can look forward and adjust itself to these spiritual forces, which can properly place before its workingmen the inducements of a united nation, a prosperous country, and fair treatment of its own people and of foreign peoples; it is the nation which can appeal to goodwill instead of to the coercive power of the army, at home and abroad; it is the nation which realizes these great spiritual forces and rids itself of purely economic and material ideals, that will in the long run win.

No nation hereafter, not even America, can live to itself alone. America has come out of the war the one great industrial power of the world. Other nations are bankrupt. America is their creditor. America has the capital, the resources, the shipping, the manpower. America may use its power as Germany tried to do. It may subsidize its capitalists and trusts and make a science of dumping. It may make other nations eventually its enemies. Or it may submit its excessive power to be regulated in partnership and equality with other free nations. The struggles of the future are industrial. The world may be governed by supply and demand, and America will win by superior control over supply. Or the world may be governed in partnership and America will take an equal chance of winning in the race of international goodwill.

REFERENCES

COMMONS, J. R., Labor and Administration, New York, (1913).

COMMONS AND ANDREWS, Principles of Labor Legislation, New York, (1916).

COMMONS AND ASSOCIATES, History of Labor in the United States, 2 vol., New York, (1918).

DEWEY, JOHN, Democracy and Education, New York, (1917).

ELY, R. T., World War and Leadership in a Democracy, New York, (1918).

ESTEY, J. A., Revolutionary Syndicalism in France, London, (1913).

GROAT, G. G., Organized Labor in America, New York, (1916).

HILQUIT, MORRIS AND RYAN, JOHN A., Socialism, Promise or Menace, New York, (1917).

HOXIE, R. F., Scientific Management and Labor, New York, (1915).

HOXIE, R. F., Trade Unionism in the United States, New York, (1917).

KELLY, R. W., Hiring the Worker, New York, (1918).

LESCOHIER, D. D., The Labor Market, New York, (1919).

Profit Sharing in the United States, Bulletin 208, U. S. Bureau of Labor Statistics, (1916).

RUBINOW, I. M., Standards of Health Insurance, New York, (1916).

SCHNEIDER, HERMAN, Education for Industrial Workers, New York, (1915).

SLICHTER, SUMNER, The Turnover of Factory Labor, New York, (1919).

Social Insurance, Proceedings of the Conference on, Bulletin 212, U. S. Bureau of Labor Statistics, (1917).

TAYLOR, FREDERICK W., The Principles of Scientific Management, New York, (1911).

WEBB, S. & B., The History of Trade Unionism, New York, (1911).

Periodicals

AMERICAN FEDERATIONIST, Washington, D. C.

MONTHLY REVIEW, U. S. Bureau of Labor Statistics

INDUSTRIAL MANAGEMENT, New York.

INDEX

A

Accidents, cause of, 52; cost of, 50, 53, 56, 59, 60; group responsibility for, 54, 55, 57, 191; and industrial insurance, 83, 89; laws for, 183; as part of industry, 56, 92, 153; prevention of, 59, 121, 152, 153; public interest in, 53, 55, 162.

Adair v. United States, *see* Law cases.

Aliens, 126.

America, place in world of, 197, 198; Revolution, 127. *See* also Labor; United States.

American Association for Labor Legislation, 97n.

American Federation of Labor, 39, 43n; authority of, 116, 117; benefits in, 83; membership of, 172; and National War Labor Board, 41, 119; Proceedings, 76n, 83n, 134n, 172n; cost of strikes in, 83; unemployment in, 76.

American Federationist, 70n.

American Labor Legislation Review, 82n.

American Labor Mission, 130.

American Statistical Association, Quarterly Publications of, 169n.

Americanization, 127–131, 163.

Anarchism, 30, 39, 102, 143, 189; in America, 195; and democracy, 37, 43, 46, 185; in Europe, 171, 174.

Annalist, 170n, 172n.

Apprenticeship, 16, 121, 136, 151, 154, 160; and education, 131–133, 135, 136; in Wisconsin, 131, 132. *See* also Continuation schools; Education.

Arbitration, board of. *See* Shop committees.

Arizona, alien law in, 126.

Arts and crafts, 144, 145.

Associations, of capital, 47, 48, 113–117, 125, 131, 178, 182; of labor, 47, 48, 113–115, 117, 125, 179, 182. *See* also Capitalism; Partnership; Trade unionism.

Austria, 188. *See* also Europe.

Autocracy, capitalism as, 195; and democracy, 40, 108; in 18th and 19th centuries, 127; in 20th century, 127, 128; theory of, 63.

D

Depression, 168–186; after 1837, 31, 171, 188, 189; after 1861, 171; after 1918, 173, 174; cycles of, 66, 71, 72, 168; and government, 184, 186; labor's share in, 68, 70, 87, 174, 176; and labor turnover, 25.

Detroit, associated employers of, 131.

Dewey, John, *Democracy and Education*, 139n, 141n.

Dicey, *Law and Opinion in England*, 37n.

Disability, 85, 86, 88–90, 95, 98, 100, 104, 191. *See* also Insurance.

Discipline, in shop, 106, 107, 122.

Division of labor, 2, 16, 144, 145, 154.

"Due process of Law," 35, 55, 109, 125, 165, 167.

Duffy, Thomas J., 91n.

"Dumping," 193, 197.

Duties, *see* Rights and duties.

E

Earnings, *see* Wages.

Education, democracy in, 136, 139; in democracy, *see* Democracy; department in industry, 155, 156; duties of, 128–131, 139, 140; in public schools, 132, 136, 138.

vocational, 132–134, 138–140, 142, 149, 150, 153–155, 190, 192; and apprenticeship, 131–133, 135, 136; characteristics of, 136, 137, 140, 141; continuation schools, 132–141; control of, 134–136, 138, 139, 142; in England, 137, 138; Federal Board for, 135n; Federal Law, 135, 138; in Germany, 135, 137, 138, 191; and school teacher, 134, 139, 156. *See* also Labor; Smith-Hughes Act; Vestibule school.

Efficiency, in industry, 72, 102, 103, 124, 140, 156, 165, 185.

"Emergency squadron," 67.

Employers, associations of, 47, 48, 113–116, 125, 131, 178, 182; as educators, 131–134; and hours of labor, 129, 130; as learners, 109; as pioneers, 29.

Employment, department, *see* Labor department.

managers, 1, 2, 88, 152, 160, 164, 166, 167; Association of Boston, 17; Conference, Proceedings of, 158n.

offices, 74, 75; federal system of, 79, 81, 185; in Ohio, 76, 77; private, 5, 77, 78, 81, 82; public, 78–81, 146; sidewalk, 2.

regularization of, 65–67, 71, 72, 81; security of, 65–73; Service Bulletin, 82n. *See* also Labor.

Engineer's theory of labor, *see* Machinery theory.

England, Chartism in, 171; Garton Foundation of, 137n; labor in, 114, 180, 181; Labor Party in, 181; legislation in, 117, 117n, 190, 192;

Parliament in, 180–182; reconstruction in, 181–183; shop committees in, 118, 119, 181, 182; and slavery, 34; and vocational education, 137, 138; in World War, 117, 117n, 118, 125, 175, 176.

English language, in industry, 131, 137; value of, 126; in Wisconsin schools, 127.

Establishment funds, 85, 87, 91, 100. *See also* Insurance.

Estey, J. A., *Revolutionary Syndicalism*, 181n.

Europe, anarchism in, 171, 174; labor in, 174, 175, 179, 187; prices and wages in, 171; revolutions in, 174, 188, 189; socialism in, 171, 174; in World War, 174, 175. *See also* Austria; France; Germany; Hungary; Italy.

F

Facts and theories, 62–64, 71, 72, 166, 167, 176, 178, 180, 185.

Federal Trade Commission, 28.

Filene, E. A., 113n.

First aid, 154.

Fisher, Irving, 92n.

Food, control of, 173.

Ford Motor Company, 18.

France, Confederation of Labor of, 181; government in, 181; Revolution, 37, 127; in World War, 125, 191, 192. *See also* Europe.

Freund, E., *Standards of American Legislation*, 47n, 56n.

Fuel Administration, 42.

G

Germany, anti-socialist law of, 191; capitalism in, 193, 194; government in, 180; and labor legislation, 190–192; policy of, 193, 197; struggles in, 188, 190; trade unionism in, 180, 189, 190; vocational education in, 135, 137, 138, 191; in World War, 125, 131, 191, 192, 195, 197. *See also* Europe.

Gide and Rist, *History of Economic Doctrines*, 56n.

Gilds, 15, 16.

Goodwill, advance in, 89, 148; and bargaining power, 19, 24, 26, 110, 115; and capitalism, 73, 178; and class harmony, 27, 28, 186; commercial, 25, 26, 28, 66; competitive persuasion, 24, 45, 46, 74, 88, 115, 145, 146; in corporation, 20, 151, 153, 154, 156, 160, 186, 192, 197; as cost, 17, 96; credit, 26; as good reputation, 18, 103; in government, 186; importance of, 28, 55, 161; industrial, 19, 26, 45, 63, 65, 67, 75, 109, 146, 148, 160, 165; from insurance, 87, 89; as intangible asset, 25, 26, 95, 96; international, 197, 198; and

P

Wilson, President, 39, 41, 43, 44, 94, 120.

Wisconsin, apprenticeship in, 131, 132; English language in, 127; hours of labor in, 29; immigration agent of, 4, 5; Industrial Commission of, 49, 50, 52, 184; Insurance Commission, 84n; laws of, 127n, 132n; Superintendent of Public Instruction, 135n; Supreme Court of, 50; workmen's compensation in, 49, 51.

Wolf, R. B., 158n.

Workmanship, instinct of, 143, 145, 149.

World Book Company, 141n.

"World, The," 187–198.

World War, and class struggle, 173, 175; and democracy, 127, 128; and England, 117, 117n, 118, 125, 175, 176; and Europe, 174, 175; Germany in, 125, 131, 191, 192, 195, 197; and health, 104; and Italy, 191, 196; and labor, 79, 81, 117; lessons of, 125, 127; National War Labor Board in, 41, 42, 70n, 117, 117n, 119, 120, 120n, 185; prices and, 169, 171; Russia in, 191, 196; and trade unionism, 195, 196.